THE PUN-DEMENTALS

The Pun-Dementals

Biblical Limericks, from Verse to Bad

DAVID C. CAMPBELL &
TIMOTHY D. CAMPBELL

RESOURCE *Publications* · Eugene, Oregon

THE PUN-DEMENTALS
Biblical Limericks, from Verse to Bad

Resource Publications
An Imprint of Wipf and Stock Publishers
199 W. 8th Ave., Suite 3
Eugene, OR 97401

www.wipfandstock.com

PAPERBACK ISBN: 978-1-6667-6007-1
HARDCOVER ISBN: 978-1-6667-6008-8
EBOOK ISBN: 978-1-6667-6009-5

MARCH 20, 2023 8:49 AM

CONTENTS

NEW TESTAMENT

APOCRYPHA

CHURCH HISTORY

PREFACE

"He that withholdeth corn, the people shall curse him, but blessing shall be upon the head of him that selleth it" (Prov 11:26 KJV). The present compilation supplies ample corn. However, less questionable exegesis can also be invoked in its support. Scripture contains numerous puns, often lost on those of us not reading the original language. In fact, some prophetic visions (*e.g.*, Jer 1:11–12) contain puns straight from God. More generally, the Bible makes use of a wide range of literary forms, not just the most refined, as a way to catch the reader's attention and convey the message. Many of the prophetic books make skilled use of different poetic styles, such as using laments both for laments and for sarcasm. Likewise, the following verses, by putting passages in unexpected and easily remembered form, may help with recalling accurate applications.

ACKNOWLEDGMENTS

SMALL PREVIOUS AUTHORS HAVE composed Old Testament[1] or church life[2] limericks. We have avoided recycling those works. Tradition describes some of the hard questions with which the Queen of Sheba tested Solomon as riddles, but in the sense of mental challenges rather than of humor. Some of the puns to follow have been around a while as jokes and riddles, but none are as old as that.

Although a few of the valid theological insights below are original, most reflect many years of listening to sermons, attending Bible studies, and reading commentaries.

Editing by Susan Campbell has been very helpful.

1. Benson, *Biblical Limericks*.
2. Clowney, *Eutychus*, 79–80.

OLD TESTAMENT

WHO'S ON FIRST?[1]

All was formless and void when begun.
Then God made the moon and the sun.
He made each living thing
And then for their king
He made Adam. That is chap one.

TIMELY ACTION[2]

God knew just the right point to say
"Let there be light," where chaos held sway:
Not unduly tarried,
Nor rushed and harried:[3]
"I'll go ahead and make My day."

---

1. Gen 1:1–27.
2. Gen 1:2–3.
3. Unlike Esau, who was hasty and who would qualify as dirty hairy.

THE AGE OF PISCES[4]

Some claim that the stars' rule can carry us,
And talk of the age of Aquarius.[5]
But each star is God's light,
And exerts no might.
No cause for astrological scary fuss.

EACH IN ITS PLACE[6]

Creatures—the LORD God made them all:
Those that swim, those that fly, walk or crawl.
Thus, the "who?" we know,
But how did it go?
For such details, on science we call.

4. Gen 1:14–18. Astrological ages refer to which constellation the equinox (point where the ecliptic and celestial equator intersect) is in. They shift with the precession of earth's axis, and move in the opposite direction to the Sun's primary motion by a degree every 72 years. The Age of Pisces lasts from ~100 BC to AD 2600 (according to the 1929 IAU constellation definitions), and is followed by the Age of Aquarius. Wikipedia says that according to various astrologers' calculations, approximate dates for entering the age of Aquarius range from 1400 to 3600, making any claims that specific great things (including technology, democracy, modernization, nervous disorders, rebellion, irresolution, world peace, Hegelianism, the replacement of religion as the opiate of the masses with the new world order-types in power, and the return of Christ to some Gnostic spiritual realm and incarnation of Ahriman) are inevitable during the age even less likely than any claim to know the date for the second coming.

5. Aquarius is the water carrier, and is followed in the position of the sun (and outer planets, ignoring retrograde motion) by Pisces, the fishes. Thus, following a man with a water jar to the site for the Last Supper (Mark 14:12–16) and subsequent development of the sign of the fish has a celestial parallel.

6. Gen 1:20–25.

SPARE RIBS?[7]

Though in Eden, something seemed amiss.[8]
Lack of sidekick[9] God would soon dismiss.
The new side effect
Had no defect!
Adam was beside himself with bliss.

ARBOR-TRARY RULE?[10]

"God said not to? Then you are not free!"
"The fruit's surely pleasant to see."
But when they broke
The law, 'twas no joke:
The command was no mere pleasant tree.

COURT OF A-PEELS[11]

"To such restrictive rules, do not cling!
Eat of this! To you it will bring
Wondrous insight
From one little bite!
It's the peach that passeth understanding."

7. Gen 2:21–23.

8. A miss was missing.

9. Although traditionally rendered "rib," the word for what God used to make Eve usually refers to the side of a building.

10. Gen 3:1–6.

11. Gen 3:4.

YES YOU CAN?[12]

"You'll find knowledge, like the pearl in a clam.
God's just gel-ous, His law's a mere sham.
This fruit you deserve!
Your power preserve!"
But in fact, we're left stuck in a jam.

STAND IN THE BREECHES[13]

Foolish autonomy was the chief
Goal of revolt; that only brought grief.
Self-trust brought them there,
Thus self-help got nowhere,[14]
Though they turned over a new leaf.

CHEATING ON THE DIET[15]

When the serpent did insinuate
That God's caring was up for debate,
Unfaithful eating
Promptly was leading
To a verdict of "in sin you ate."

---

12. Gen 3:4–6.

13. Gen 3:5–7. "Breeches" is the Geneva Bible's distinctive translation of the foliage-based attire.

14. No wear was also part of the problem.

15. Gen 3:1–11.

NO-FAULT INSURANCE[16]

They tried to pass fault on and on.
He blamed her; she sought to hand on
Blame to the snake,
Who got no break
Because he had no leg to stand on.

RELEGATED TO A FOOTNOTE[17]

He's guilty, no chance for appeal.
Judgment the serpent soon will feel,
Crushing his head,
For he's de-feet-ed.
Surely Satan will be brought to heel.

FUTURE PRESENT[18]

A new covenant they receive:
Not of works, but by grace they believe.
The spiritual rift
Will be crossed by a gift—
The promise of a Christmas Eve.

16. Gen 3:8–14.
17. Gen 3:14–15.
18. Gen 3:15.

IN A MIRROR, DIMLY[19]

The unfallen world's gone, alas.
Humanity the test did not pass.
Although we now see
Hints of divinity,
God's image is now a stained glass.

HEARTBREAK[20]

There's now conflict with the other gender,
Garden blocked by a heavenly defender;
Through lack of heedin'
We have lost Eden:
Address unknown, return to cinder.[21]

MUTINY[22]

Though the garden was free from all pain,
Adam and Eve chose a vain
Rebellion instead;
To death it led;
Then they promptly began raising Cain.

---

19. Gen 3:16–23.

20. Gen 3:16–24.

21. The phrase "ashes to ashes" was an expansion on "dust to dust" in the Book of Common Prayer, well before Elvis.

22. Gen 3:1—4:1. cf. Humphrey Bogart's naval film role.

CANDID CAIN[23]

Cain's selfishness is justly fabled,
For through chutzpah he was enabled
After the crime
To whine, "This time,
By the curse I'm unfairly dis-abeled!"

NOT SO WELLS[24]

Repentance he viewed with disdain:
"I'll build my way out of this bane!
From curse, immunity
Through my community!
In my town, I'll be Citizen Cain."

INHERITANCE[25]

To work out the numbers many tried:
Add them up? Can some patterns be spied
In the digits?[26]
Don't give yourself fits:
The point's not subtle: "and he died."

---

23. Gen 4:6–14.

24. Gen 4:9–17. It was a war of the worldly.

25. Gen 5:1–32.

26. As biblical genealogies focus on showing connection rather than exhaustive enumeration, gaps are common. The Septuagint, Samaritan, and Masoretic texts have large differences in the numbers of years in Genesis 5 and 11, illustrating the difficulty of copying a lot of numbers accurately. The numbers have various statistical peculiarities, which may reflect not being originally intended as actual years. As the Bible never comments on the numbers, and in fact warns against undue preoccupation with genealogies (1 Tim 1:4), getting caught up in issues of dates is unlikely to be helpful.

A CALCULATED RESPONSE[27]

To build a ship needs math talents.[28]
Trigonometry was in evidence:
The waves' conjunction
Was a sin function;[29]
Naps on deck made them ark tan gents.

HONEY HAM?[30]

'Midst flooding, to save all their lives:
Cabins each: Noah, sons, and their wives;
The animals all
Got a suitable stall;
And the bees were in the ark hives.

ARK DEBARK[31]

The raven left first, it is reckoned.
Then the dove clearly went out second.[32]
We have no word
On who went third,
But the rest all went forth, and were fecund.

---

27. Gen 6:14–16.

28. Shem, Ham, and Japheth, on seeing their father tally up how much fodder to load on board, observed, "There's Noah counting for tastes."

29. The way every angle of evil multiplied was a sine of the times.

30. Gen 6:14–22.

31. Gen 8:6–19.

32. The dove's second return was a re-leaf.

BABBLE ON AND ON[33]

Looking down, God could plainly see that
Their stairway to heaven would fall flat.[34]
A mere foolish joke
That would vanish like smoke
Even if they'd built packs of ziggurats.[35]

SISTER ACT[36]

Critics say "It's one tale, garbled thrice.
For man's wisdom is always so nice
That a father's error
Isn't made by heir, nor
Would one do a foolish thing twice."

OUTCASTING LOT[37]

The Jordan valley looked best to him,
But prospects for good neighbors were grim.
Soon the cities were done,
And as for each son,
Later we will hear Mo-ab-out them.

---

33. Gen 11:1–9.

34. Misled Zepplin? Their unity was an example of sinner-gy.

35. On the Tigris-Euphrates floodplain, a sacrifice on top of a step pyramid would be obvious for miles, hence the observation that smoking ziggurats are bad for your stealth.

36. Gen 12:11–20; 20:2–18; 26:6–11.

37. Gen 13, 14, 19.

NOT JUST FOSTER CHILDREN[38]

"You've promised, but how can this be?"
Through a vision, the LORD made him see:
"After some duress,
Your heirs will have success."
Then Abe said "I dream of genealogy."[39]

RIGHTLY DIVIDING[40]

To forestall disobedient strife,
The sacrifice went under the knife:
There is no short cut,
No if, and, or but,
No evasion, in this slice of life.

SPEAK OF ARABY[41]

Motherhood did not make Hagar meeker,
But that made her prospects seem bleaker.
"You are not done;
God will bless your son.
He will be a mover and sheiker."

---

38. Gen 15:2–16.

39. Given typical Mediterranean-area complexions, some of them may have been light brown heirs.

40. Gen 15:8–18.

41. Gen 16.

MELODY MALADY[42]

When fulfillment seemed long delayed,
Sarah's hopes proceeded to fade.
The laughter the LORD hears:
Not music to His ears,
Though an instance of Sarah nayed.

OUT, OUT![43]

The warning seemed merely a whim,
'Til the margin of escape wore thin.
Getting out of Sodom
Didn't get to the bottom
Of the problem—get Sodom out of them.

OUT STANDING[44]

From temptation, we have no immunity;
Worldly influences seize each opportunity.
It will be our fault
If we fall to a salt,
Becoming a pillar of the community.

---

42. Gen 18:10–15.
43. Gen 19:12–32.
44. Gen 19:26.

MAKING THE CALCULATIONS[45]

God called upon Abraham.
His son would sub for a lamb.
It was a hard route;
Abe couldn't compute
Until God supplied him with RAM.

A SPELL OF TROUBLE?[46]

If 'twere alphabet soup, I allege
That it would have taken off hunger's edge.
"My hunting's been tough!
Gimme some read stuff!"
Trading birthwrite for a pot of message.[47]

GRASPING THE SITUATION[48]

Trouble clearly was brewing
For Jacob, but 'twas his own doing.
He swiped the blessing
By devious dressing
When Esau already was stewing.[49]

---

45. Gen 22:1–13.

46. Gen 25:29–34.

47. Esau didn't exactly eat his words, but he did manage to swallow his pride by the time Jacob returned from his time with Laban.

48. Gen 25:29–34; 27:1–29.

49. Clearly, the mess of pottage was not appease pudding. For Jacob, having Rebekah cook the game-flavored stew was outsaucing. Isaac's request for roast game suggests a pottage dotage.

HOLE-Y WAR?[50]

Of a conflict we must now tell.
Does Isaac at Gerar ring a bell?
Abimelech's men
Quarreled with him.
Don't you know why? Well, well, well.[51]

THE MORE, THE WEARIER[52]

If two become one, then we see
That there's problems with polygamy.
Esau's three tries
Weren't very wise.
His Basemath should have been binary.

A LADDER-NIGHT SAINT[53]

Jacob strayed, yet God would keep
A watch on His quite errant sheep.
And when the fellow
Needed a pillow,
He was duly rocked to sleep.

50. Gen 26:18–22.

51. Later, when Abimelech sought a covenant, he told Isaac that those who quarreled merely artesian him.

52. Gen 26:34–35; 36:1–3. It's not clear how the names as given in 26:34 and 36:2–18 match up; if two wives had the same name it would not be surprising if alternatives were also used.

53. Gen 28:11–12.

DOUBLE RING CEREMONY[54]

Of many sons Rachel did dream,
Thinking that they'd raise her esteem.
But quite a mess'll
Come when you wrestle;
Trouble came when she tried a tag team.

TAKING STOCK OF THE SITUATION[55]

Rachel, Leah: they did both vote
To leave, for they could quickly note
What was plain to see:
Dad was not happy,
For Jacob had gotten Laban's goat.

HIP REPLACEMENT[56]

To many ploys, Jacob did resort
Yet they all proved to come up short.
Wrestling the LORD
A lesson did afford:
True success must be a joint effort.

54. Gen 30:7–8.
55. Gen 31.
56. Gen 32:24–32.

DEAL BREAKER[57]

Trusting grace is not how he'd begun.
Rights, wives, flocks—always more to be won:
Clawing to the top
With every swap,
But Jack of all trades is made Master's son.

FOLLOWING THE HERD[58]

With neighbors they so freely mixed,
That God's plan seemed to be nearly nixed.
So the Lord shipped
Them to Egypt.
Poimenophobia[59] the mingling fixed.

A HARD CELL[60]

Joseph in the dungeon had his berth.
But on dreams he was the best on earth.
The cupbearer released
But the baker deceased
As Pharaoh took back his leaven's worth.[61]

---

57. Gen 35:1–3.
58. Gen 38; 46:31–14.
59. Poimen (Greek): a shepherd.
60. Gen 40:1–22.
61. A major penitentiary was located at Leavenworth, Kansas.

CAUTION: SLIPPERY WHEN MISINTERPRETED[62]

"My Asher will have royal riches,
Dip his foot into olive oil," is
Not a tribe's foot-shaped soil,
Nor pipelines for oil.
One might call that bad Exxon-gesis.

WRAPPING UP[63]

Joseph died in Egypt, it is true.
But he knew that God would see them through.
Hence his final demand:
"Take my bones to the land"—
Thus a patriarch and mummy too.

SINK OR SWIM?[64]

The Hebrews multiplied with such vim,
Pharaoh sought to toss sons in the swim.
The slaves might rebel!
So the unrest to quell,[65]
He sought to a-Nile-ate them.

---

62. Gen 49:20. A rather creative interpreter claimed that Jacob's blessing that Asher would "dip his foot in oil" was a prophecy of the future territory of his tribe being vaguely foot-shaped with an oil pipeline running through it.

63. Gen 50:24–26.

64. Exod 1:9–22.

65. Perhaps the first pre-quell.

WRONGLY DIVIDING[66]

Where reeds on the river bank bordered,
Discovery of a child was recorded.
An account we see
Split in JPED,
Thus Moses is drawn out—and quartered. [67]

LIGHTING THE WAY[68]

Life in Egypt was that of a wretch,
But the Hebrews did little but kvetch.
Still, God had a plan:
"I know just the man!
With shrubbery Moses I'll fetch."[69]

NOT JUST A DAIRY TALE[70]

Canaan with milk and honey flows;
God's generous providence shows.
From this we can see:
It's a good place to bee,
Udder delight its resident knows.

---

66. Exod 2:1–10.

67. Replacing Mosaic origins with mosaic origins for the text.

68. Exod 2:23—3:3.

69. A bit like the knights who say "Nee!," Gilliam and Jones, *Grail*.

70. Exod 3:8.

HANDLE WITH CARE[71]

God showed Moses one snake and one robe trick.
To the snake his response was aerobic.
In the adrenaline rush
Moe forgot the bush.
Would that Eve were as herpetophobic!

FEAT OF CLAY[72]

In a straw poll, the Hebrews would say:
"We've drawn short straws for many a day!"
Now Pharaoh's argument
Was a straw man. They went
To Moe, saying, "That's the last straw![73] Hay!"

WARTS AND ALL[74]

When the land with anurans did crawl,
Pharaoh on his magicians did call.
They hopped to it,
But doing their bit
Helped not—of woes upped the toadal.[75]

---

71. Exod 4:1–7.

72. Exod 5:4–21.

73. Although here the problem was too little straw, later Israel got in trouble with baals.

74. Exod 8:1–15.

75. Soon the frogs all croaked. The name Hophni means "tadpole," cf. "Tadpole" Phelps, whom Dr. Watson chased with a cricket bat in his youth, several years before he met Sherlock Holmes (Doyle, "Naval Treaty," 305).

LETTING GO[76]

The magicians had long ceased to smile.
They'd known that they'd lost, for a while.
But release was not yet,
For Pharaoh was all wet,
Stubbornly he stayed in denile.

FALL WEATHER[77]

The Hebrews sought for some relief,
But Pharaoh was stubborn past belief.
In his great pride,
He wished to preside,
So they played "Hail to the Chief."[78]

DON'T TRUST THE GPS[79]

These people are but newly sown.
They need time for their skills to hone.
So a short northern route
Just wouldn't suit.
Go through Succoth—no passing Zoan.[80]

---

76. Exod 8:19.

77. Exod 9:18–35.

78. In Pharaoh's opinion, Moses was raising hail.

79. Exod 13:17–18.

80. Zoan, the Hebrew name for Tanis, was a little north of Rameses, the starting point of the exodus. Rameses was abandoned not long after the exodus, with reusable building materials incorporated into Tanis, hence Ps. 78 referring to the area of Zoan rather than to the then no longer existing Rameses. The short northern route was well-fortified by the Egyptians, thus a bad route for the fleeing people (Kitchen, *Reliability*, 255–6).

A SEA AND A STAFF OF REEDS[81]

After the last Israelite started,
The chariots after them darted.
But the heaven-sent wind
Soon came to an end;
Sea and horsemen were both de-parted.

THE RIGHT SOLUTION[82]

Through semi-permeable barrier they were sent
By os-Moses, that much is evident.
Which ones go through
Can be found by you
In the consecration gradient.[83]

GO NORTHEAST VERY CIRCUITOUSLY, YOUNG PEOPLE[84]

The Hebrews were not all the best.
Many would fail at the test.
But the time was at hand
To inherit the land:
Their destiny was manna fest.

81. Exod 14:15–28; Isa 36:6.

82. Exod 14.

83. Osmosis is the process where water diffuses through a barrier (such as a cell membrane) that blocks the passage of some other molecules and ions. More water will move from where there is a higher proportion of water to the other side; counteracting this requires active use of energy at the molecular level. Likewise, the natural trend for humanity is to move towards the less consecrated side.

84. Exod 16:4–7.

ABHORRED HOARD[85]

"God's providence, you can now see.
He'll provide food abundantly."
Not using their noodles,
They sought to keep oodles,
And had to admit "Manna caught me."[86]

MAINTAINING THE CHARGE[87]

Moses was the first person to get
A data download from cloud to tablet.
"That law needs an update!"
Of such claims, there's a spate,
But it's my thoughts needing refreshed, I would bet.

HEAR, O ISRAEL![88]

"Who can hear God's voice and live?"
They were right, this respect to give.
Yet in a deeper way,
Peter was right to say,
We can't not hear His word and live.

---

85. Exod 16:19–20.

86. A piece of pasta understanding? (Phil 4:7, KJV)

87. Exod 20.

88. Exod 20:19; John 6:68.

NO CHISELERS[89]

To sacrifice aright, one must know
It is grace, and not one's own show.
You must build alone
With undressed stone
To deflate any altar ego.

STING OPERATION[90]

That the LORD fights for you, you will know,
For hornets before you will go.[91]
They should be abuzz
With what the LORD does,
But instead, they keep bugging Moe.

DIAGNOSIS[92]

His care the people were scorning,
So God gave promise and warning
By inscribing
His prescribing:
"Take these tablets; call Me every morning."

89. Exod 20:25.

90. Exod 23:28.

91. Perhaps foreshadowing drone warfare. Whether this is literal insects or symbolized human foes is debated.

92. Exod 32:15–16.

NO BULL PRIZE[93]

Many people's commitment was half-
Hearted, just seeking a laugh.
At Sinai their party[94]
Became so hearty,
That Moses made them drink de calf.[95]

A CATTLE-LOG OF RULES[96]

The sin offering's totally
Burnt up, and a bull, it must be.
But for peace offering,
A cow you may bring,
And it's shared: heifer God, heifer me.

SPLIT THE DIFFERENCE[97]

Offerings, if we are thoughtful,
Cannot sway God, and cannot earn pull.
To fix our own sin
We can't even begin,
But from this we see sin's tear a bull.

93. Exod 32:1–20.

94. A sinner re-veal party.

95. How does Moses make this beverage? Hebrews it.

96. Lev 3:1–5; 4:3–21.

97. Lev 4:1–21.

PICKY EATERS[98]

Skeptics scoff, "So, God's unaware
That rabbits don't chew cud?"[99] But where
We just have a way
To tell what food's OK,
We should learn not to split a hare.

CHECK THE STALLS[100]

What should we on the table be putting
To show that we heed God in our cooking?
Perhaps a boar?
Check cud, hooves for sure.
So now bring us some piggy footing.[101]

BIRD GUIDE[102]

For big things that fly in the air,
Of carnivores, you should beware.
Eating an owl
Would be very foul,
But for others, we see: fowl is fare.[103]

---

98. Lev 11:3–8.

99. Rabbits and hyraxes (called rock badgers or coneys in some translations) do not produce true cud in the technical sense that cows, deer, antelope, and camels do; however, they do sit around chewing in a similar manner, with similar function, close enough for a non-biologist to lump the behaviors together.

100. Lev 11:7.

101. We won't know until we get some, so bring it right here.

102. Lev 11:13–19.

103. The witches in *Macbeth* had somewhat similar comments.

THE GERM OF AN IDEA[104]

In our superior modern knowledge we bask
As we take the ancients to task:
"Tell us now, if you please
Why it might slow disease[105]
If you distance and put on a mask?"

HOME SICK[106]

Leprosy in a house, to our eyes,
Seems silly, but in fact this law's wise.
Toxic mold? Throw it out!
Do not be a lout
And sell it to some other guys.[107]

IN-GRAINED HABITS[108]

Although such labor could be tough,
And would not always yield lots of stuff,
Folks could grapefully take
Gleanings left for their sake.
They could gather just barley enough.

---

104. Lev 13:45–46.

105. The disease called leprosy today (Hansen's disease) does not closely match the symptoms described in the Old Testament for the ailments requiring quarantine.

106. Lev 14:34–53.

107. Neither actual mold nor spiritual rot is solved by putting up a wall to hide it, either.

108. Lev 19:9–10.

MARKED? OUT!¹⁰⁹

These laws are not mere odd whims:
With idolatrous meaning it brims.
A heathen tattoo
Is clearly taboo;
Cut out any pagan-style trims.¹¹⁰

CAMP TOWN PLACES¹¹¹

From their start until time to park,
The Gershonites with curtains embark;
The Merarite boasts
Of carrying posts;
The Kohathites were aiders of the ark.

SOMETHING TO CRY ABOUT¹¹²

Hearing so many moans melon-choly,
Moses felt like an overworked collie.
"We've had no leeks
For many long weeks!"
Whiners—rapscallions in their folly.

---

109. Lev 19:27–28.
110. Jer 25:23 shows that this was a Buz cut.
111. Num 4.
112. Num 11:4–15.

SHORT CIRCUIT[113]

"That the land is good we saw quickly:
Of produce we had our pick. We
Found the land runny
With milk and with honey,
But giants![114] That makes things sticky!"

CUT OFF FROM THE VINE[115]

The spies found Canaan's produce in line
With promise, and Eschol most fine.
But it was a raisinable hunch
They'd be an ungrapeful bunch
And ten spies gave nothing but whine.

SLAM-DUNK ARGUMENT[116]

To trust God and embolden were the aims,
But they sowed dissent with wild claims:
"Those folks are so tall!
They all play basketball!
We think that we saw HeBron James!"

---

113. Num 13.

114. They saw the Anakim and went over to the dark side.

115. Num 13.

116. Num 13.

OH BRETHREN![117]

Many claimed the Hebrew label,
The good all mixed up with the rabble.
Refining took 40 years,
And myriad tears,
Until they were Canaan-able.

INHERIT THE WHINE[118]

You and Egypt know which God is boss;
Through reed sea[119] you safely crossed;
I gave manna, water,
And law and order;
Yet you fear premature heir loss?

FLOURY PROSE[120]

For God's gifts we should give thanks and praise.
Faithful tithing is one of the ways.
From this verse we know:
We should give of our dough;
Giving more every time there's a raise.

117. Num 14:22–45.

118. Num 14:22–31.

119. "Sea of Reeds" is geographically more accurate than Red Sea for the location of the Hebrew escape. This does not diminish the effectiveness of the miraculous intervention at stopping pursuit, nor the ingratitude of promptly presuming that God can't help with other difficulties.

120. Num 15:17–21.

HEM NO. 1[121]

A fringe on your cloak is a way
To remember the LORD every day.
But don't make a hassle
About your tassel—
Look to God, keep above the fray.

CENSER-SHIP[122]

Rebellion from murmurs did condense,
Korah sought his men to convince:
"We're God's people too!"—
That much was true.
"We'll usurp priestly jobs!" was noncense.

STAFF MEETING[123]

The rebels' claim was such a divisor,
That Jacob risked having no survivor.
But the sign of the rod
Was clearly from God,
Now the people are sadder, bud wiser.

121. Num 15:37–39.
122. Num 16:1–40.
123. Num 16:41—17:13.

THE JAWBONE OF AN ASS[124]

After Sihon and Og, 'twas no doubt
Versus Israel Balak faced a rout.
So with Midian's aid,
Much cash he paid
For a prophet to come bail 'im out.

PAVED WITH BAD INTENTIONS[125]

When his steed made a sudden halt,
Balaam commenced an assault.
Like drivers today
Who blame the roadway,
Balaam thought it was the ass's fault.[126]

DONKEY OUGHTIE[127]

Balak's big payout he hoped to count,
But his steed, of good sense proved a fount.
The pacemaking, odd,
Because she saw God,
Led to the Sermon from the Mount.

124. Num 22:2–21.

125. Num 22:22–33.

126. Based on the Scottish translation, paving may have been invented by Seth, as he was MacAdam.

127. Num 22:22–33.

PLACE DE L'ÉTOILE QUI SORT DE JACOB[128]

The mighty will shrivel and parch
As they reach gates of Death on life's march.
By His death Christ bought
Death's claim and then wrought
Hell's gates into triumphal arch.

FOLLOW THE DIRECTIONS[129]

"Your parents would not heed, you see.
They roamed in this desert forty
Years for their crime.
Please listen this time!"
Moe's review gave us Deuteronomy.

CAUTION IN THE COUNTRY[130]

From temptation the land's no oasis.
Pagan ties will not produce stasis.
Syncretism creeps in
And lures you to sin
There's trouble from friends in high places.[131]

---

128. Num 24:17; 1 Cor 15:55. "Place of the Star," popular designation of the location of the Arc de Triomphe in Paris; "*qui sort de*" = who comes out of.

129. Deut 1–11.

130. Deut 7:1–5.

131. The dark side of this might suggest Darth Brooks.

PREVENT THE UPSET[132]

Life in Canaan will be easier,
But do not let complacency seize ya!
You must never forget
From Whom you did get
The blessings—avoid milk of amnesia.

DON'T GET THE BIRD[133]

From compromise, you must desist.
Syncretism? Always resist.
Act as they do?
Judged like them, too!
Parrot them, you're a polly theist.

EASY AS PIE[134]

Follow God and walk in His light;
Do not condone any heathen rite.
If the moon hits your eye,
And you bow to the sky,
Then you surely will die—it's Amorite.

---

132. Deut 8:11–20.
133. Deut 12:29–32.
134. Deut 17:3.

THE GLORY WILL DEPART[135]

Folks will say "Give us a king!" but then
He'll become tyrannical when
Big herds of steeds
Serve greed, not needs:
Better to just have horseless headmen.

HAREM-SCAREM[136]

The once-mighty charger now drags;
A young face soon wrinkles and sags;
Earthly riches rust.
In the LORD you must trust,
Or be stuck with a bunch of old nags.

WANDERING ARAMEANS[137]

Self-centered, stubborn—how could that be?
Ungrateful when God's care was plain to see!
To lovingkindness divine,
They replied with a whine.
How foolish! How oft that's like me!

135. Dt. 17:16. Cf. 1 Sam 4:21; Irving, "Sleepy Hollow", 457; Wodehouse, "Ukridge's Dog College", 14.

136. Deut 17:16–17.

137. Dt. 26:5.

COUNTING BLESSINGS IN THE FAT OF THE LAND[138]

Far too often, we are quite slow
To give all of the thanks that we owe.
Olive-covered hills,
From which oil spills?
Don't forget to count Monte Crisco.[139]

YOUR SANDAL HAS NOT WORN OUT[140]

From spring rain and snowmelt water poured in.
The flood was far too deep for fordin'.
But, thanks to God,
They crossed dry-shod.
No dunking, though they had air Jordan.

RAHAB REHAB[141]

Chaos monster or innkeeper in view?
Was Rahab named when she was two?
Though chaos can start in
A kindergarten,
They are not the same word in Hebrew.

138. Dt. 32:13.

139. It's easy to slip up in this regard, and even easier to slip down.

140. Josh 3:13–17.

141. Josh 2:1; Ps. 89:10.

CIRCUIT RIDER[142]

Rounding the walls with God's protection
Conquered all (save for Rahab's defection).
Those now circling cities,
Sounding horns and not ditties,
Are on a bypass, with bad direction.

SIEGE PERILOUS[143]

The Canaanites sought out no aid
When Joshua's visit was paid,
But their trusted wall
Proceeded to fall
As if by low bidder made.

PATCHED RELATIONSHIPS[144]

Most Canaanites to hostility did hold,
But Gibeonites were crafty and bold.
Their bread, it was seen
Was dried up and green.
From resistance, they broke the mold.[145]

142. Josh 6:1–23.

143. Josh 6.

144. Josh 9.

145. This presaged the Israelites' later tendency to fall into the error of thinking that acting like the Canaanites would make them fun guys.

TAKES THE CAKE[146]

The Israelites the supplies did view;
Did not ask the LORD, "Is it true?"
It seemed quite clear
That Gibeon was not near:
"Eat? Archaic! And habit, too."

SHADOW OF THE ALMIGHTY[147]

Joshua prayed that the sun
Would be blocked. Thus battle was won.
A cloud far out of season
Was the miraculous reason.
Far before even SPF 1.[148]

VACANT LOTS[149]

A few tribes, of zeal, are a hot bed,
But "Me next!" by the rest was not said.
The slacking tribes ought
To start casting lots,
For a lot of lots weren't yet allotted.

---

146. Josh 9.

147. Josh 10:12–14.

148. Solar Protection Factor for sunblock. This passage is commonly taken to describe the sun standing still, but the Hebrew word can refer to being terminated rather than a pause in motion. Given the climate and time of year, blocking the sun would likely be more conducive of prolonged fighting than would a lengthened period of heat. Such an unusual cloud might have been connected by the Israelites to the cloud of God's presence during the Exodus. The interpretation is not certain; another idea is asking for an unfavorable astrological sign to dismay the Canaanites. The urban legend associated with "Joshua's long day" is well-discussed by Harvey, *Joshua*.

149. Josh 18:3.

DON'T LET THE RIGHT HAND KNOW[150]

Ehud devised a daring plan;
Thus revolt versus Moab began.
Eglon didn't infer
Anything sinister;
He thought Ehud his right-hand man.[151]

A MODEL T OF BRAVERY?[152]

What had seemed invincible hordes,
No longer are they overlords!
Invaders lost their drive,
Quickly they ceased to strive,
For Israelites had seized the fords.[153]

THE RAIN ON THE PLAIN[154]

Barak feared that he'd surely fail,
But God vanquished with thunder and hail.
With his chariot stuck,
Sisera—out of luck—
Was sent quite directly to Jael.[155]

---

150. Judg 3:15–21.

151. He was probably relying on secondhand information.

152. Judg 3:26–30.

153. This contrasts with speculation about connections between Zoroastrianism and Judaism, with the former's belief in Ahura Mazda.

154. Judg 4–5.

155. When Jael pegged him as an enemy, Sisera learned how much was at stake in the battle. He did not pass go nor collect 200 shekels nor any other booty. The refreshment might suggest that Heber was a milk sheik.

NO WOOL OVER HIS EYES[156]

He received orders from the Lord, yet
To verify his calling, a test's set.
Gideon was sure
No dew-it-yourselfer
Alone could ever make a dew, wet.

JARRING EXPERIENCE[157]

The row shocked them from the mists
Of sleep. "Foes in camp!" their fear hissed.
What could the noise be?
Terror of mystery!
For they were not racket scientists.[158]

NIGHT STAND[159]

Gideon took directions well.
The foes were scattered pell-mell.
Not one Midianite
Remained the next night
Not even in any hotel.[160]

---

156. Judg 6:36–40.

157. Judg 7:17–22

158. Gideon's skill in wielding a racket brings to mind other tennis greats like Joseph, who served in Pharaoh's courts.

159. Judg 7.

160. After all, the Gideons would have found them there.

THIRST FOR JUSTICE[161]

Once his parable brought Abimelech down,
Jotham fled, his trouble to drown
For we read here,
That he fled to Beer.
No, no! That's the name of the town.

A SLIP OF THE LISP[162]

Though in looks, the lines might be blurred,
By their speech the test was assured.
They couldn't restrain
Saying "ear of grain."[163]
Thus they're caught by a simple passhword.

STRONG WORDS[164]

The LORD said, "You'll have a son."
Manoah cried, "We are undone!"
His wife said, "Don't be silly!
Think about it, really!
We've a task that we haven't begun."

161. Judg 9:7–21.
162. Judg 12:1–6.
163. Shibboleth.
164. Judg 13.

QUENCHING A THIRST FOR KNOWLEDGE[165]

To his Philistine buddies, he addresses
A riddle that eludes all their guesses.
It will cost money
To not guess honey
As the clue to the paws that refreshes.

DON'T FIDDLE WITH THE RIDDLE[166]

They tried, but the quest kept defyin'
Their wits. So they set the bride cryin'.
"With my heifer you plow?
I'll get you somehow!"
When they could pre-empt his punched lion.

FOX IN SHOCKS[167]

Angry, Samson went home in spite,
Then a stand-in gave him no delight.
They sought a break,
But revenge he did take:
Outfoxing them with taillights.

165. Judg 14:8–14. Cf. Judg 15:19.
166. Judg 14:12–18.
167. Judg 14:19—15:5.

A JAWBREAKER, ANYONE?[168]

Bashing Philistines is what he does,
When he comes, he makes quite a buzz.[169]
One day he pronounced,
"A thousand I've trounced!"
And what a jaw-dropper that was.

EMERGENCY EXIT[170]

The Philistines feared Samson's might
But thought they had trapped him one night.
Samson did not tarry
But instead he did carry
His departure gate onto his flight.[171]

THE TIES THAT BIND[172]

Everything that Delilah did say
Was a ploy, just to get her own way.
"What's your favorite hymn?"
She'd respond with vim:
"It's an old one: Truss and Disobey."

---

168. Judg 15:15–17.

169. As opposed to the buzz cut received a bit later.

170. Judg 16:2–3.

171. Like many later travelers, Sampson was also known to have a snack packed in his carrion.

172. Judg 16:11–12.

FROM AN ANTIQUE LAND[173]

Her greed should have caused him great gloom,
But he failed to perceive his near doom.
Why would she weave
Such a web to deceive?
Let him smash a cherished hair loom?[174]

BRUNETTE BOMBSHELL?[175]

Delilah to the reward kept aspirin',
While Samson, from the whinin', was tirin'.
"Philistines—upon you!"
Turned out to be true.
The very first known hair raid siren.

SLAVE AND A HAIRCUT[176]

Samson let lust be his master.
With Delilah he tried living faster.
His judgment did fail
In this hair-razing tale,
As he took a short cut to disaster.

---

173. Judg 16:13–14.

174. Going for the dis-tressed look.

175. Judg 16:15–21.

176. Judg 16:4–21. The offered reward of 1100 pieces of silver from each Philistine lord was rather more than two bits.

INTO THE RING[177]

Her nagging served Delilah well,
Taking its toll until Samson fell.
It was their last round;
Soon he was bound,
For Samson was shaved by the belle.[178]

CLOSING ACT[179]

They thought Samson's strength would stay gone.[180]
So they gave him the floor to play on.
But instead of playing clown,
He brought the house down,
And as for the audience—Dagon.

HE DID IT MICAH'S WAY[181]

"Surely God can't contain His delight!
Now I'm doing everything right!
Theft and idolatry,
Shrine and priest made by me,
And I have a genuine Levite!"

177. Judg 16:4–21.

178. Indirectly; she prudently had someone else do the barber-ous deed. For Samson, this barbershop duet was the barber of un-civil.

179. Judg 16:22–30.

180. Actually, his strength re-maned.

181. Judg 17:2–13.

600 BRIDES FOR 600 TRIBESMEN[182]

From "judge" to "restore" concern passes,
But unvowed maidens aren't found in masses.
Hiding in a bush,
Quite syrup-titious,
Allowed them to obtain mo' lasses.[183]

NAOMI OR MARA[184]

She felt, to tell the truth, less
Pleasant than bitter and useless:
Her husband done,
The death of each son,
But at least she wasn't ruthless.

OUT IN RIGHT FIELD[185]

For the future she could be afraid.
Her sister in Moab had stayed.
But the faithful Ruth
Pursued the truth
And won a beau, as she obeyed.

182. Judg 21:16–23.

183. Although Song of Songs suggests this can be sweet, Jacob, Elkanah, and Solomon found that too much led to sticky situations (cf. Job 42:14).

184. Ruth 1.

185. Ruth 1:6—3:13.

WHO'S WHO?[186]

Does he want to claim the land? He does;
But he just cannot do so, because:
"To preserve my name,
I can't take the dame."
Now we do not know what his name was.

NO MAN CAN SERVE TWO MASTERS[187]

From bigamy Elkanah got strife.
Hannah had a sad, bitter life.
"In me you did win
More than sons ten,"
Failed to cheer a purpose-driven wife.[188]

THE CALL OF THE LORD[189]

Though Samuel is still small in size,
To answer well, how often he tries.
Until Eli did see
The caller ID—
But the number that was up was Eli's.

186. Ruth 4:1–7.
187. 1 Sam 1.
188. Heavy-hearted Hannah, the wife of Elkanah.
189. 1 Sam 3:1–14.

WHO COMES OUT AHEAD?[190]

On ritual Israel made a stand,
But the army would soon be unmanned.
Though His priests were dead,
The Lord stayed ahead,
With Dagon forced to give God a hand.

EKRON JONES AND THE TABERNACLE OF DOOM[191]

The plagues and mice made their mark.
God's bite worse than Israel's bark.
Each Philistine town
Turned the offer down,
As the raiders sought to lose the ark.

A DASHING LEADER[192]

The meeting seemed mere chance on the road,
But Samuel knew what it would bode.
So he did choose
To give Saul time to muse:
In public, anointing used morsel code.

190. 1 Sam 4:5–11; 5:1–5.

191. 1 Sam 5:6—6:2.

192. 1 Sam 9:19—10:8. The Israelites thought that he looked dashing, but regrettably, Saul later became dotty.

TALL SAUL[193]

For height, not for being wise,
Israel thought that Saul was a prize,
But along came Goliath,
And now the king sigheth:
"Pick on someone further from your own size!"

AN AYE FOR AN EYE[194]

The naysayers got into a snit:
"To save us, Saul's surely not fit!"
Beating the Ammonites
Gave most people delights.
After that, it was clear the eyes had it.

RAPPEL REPEL[195]

Philistines thought that their might would prevail
To teach Jonathan that he'd surely fail.
"They're little moles
To chase back into holes"—
Belittling the size of his faith's scale.[196]

193. 1 Sam 10:23–24; 17:4–11.
194. 1 Sam 10:27—11:13.
195. 1 Sam 14:1–15.
196. A cliffhanger.

RAPPEL REPEL SEQUEL[197]

Saul foolishly sought new directive
When he should have been firmly executive.
Then with a rash vow,
He thought he could wow
God, with blessing a wow consecutive.[198]

DOOM RAIDERS[199]

Each Amalekite marauding band
Must be driven out of the land.
To apply this today,
We might well say
Many bands belong under the ban.

A LOWING BLOW[200]

"We needn't obey God's clear line;
Sacrifices will surely be fine.
That's what we'll do!"
But Samuel knew,
To err is human; to moo is bovine.[201]

---

197. 1 Sam 14:16–46.

198. Hebrew grammar pun from Clowney, *Eutychus*, 47.

199. 1 Sam 15:2–3.

200. 1 Sam 15:14.

201. Saul's excuse that the people made him do it was cow-word-ly.

TAKE OUT[202]

Since anointment, not much seems to come by.
"With this bread, to your brothers now fly—
With extra cheese;"[203]
It seems that he's
Just a pita delivery guy.

EWES-FUL EXPERIENCE[204]

Invective his patience was tryin',
For Goliath did not cease defyin',
But failed at scaring:
Dave's confident bear-ing
Showed upon Whom he's re-lion.

SIZING UP THE SITUATION[205]

"God's might gives true security.
To face the foe I am ready.
No need of big armor
To keep me from harm, for
God's providence fits perfectly."

202. 1 Sam 17:17–30.

203. Eliab accused David of treating the chance to see the battle as a feta attraction.

204. 1 Sam 17:34–36.

205. 1 Sam 17:31–39.

NOT THINKING A HEAD[206]

Goliath came out with a roar.
He thought he'd slay foes by the score.
But then, what a shock!
Just one smallish rock—
Never entered his mind before.

ILL-BREAD REMARKS[207]

Goliath scoffed, "What's this I see?
You think that I'm just a puppy?
I'll feed you to the birds!"
Such were his proud words.
David countered, "You wanna pita me?"

WORSHIP WARS[208]

Saul sought music to calm his fear,
But interrupted David with a spear.
Now, when some strum the strings,
The sound that it brings
Makes others wish a javelin near.

206. 1 Sam 17:40–50.
207. 1 Sam 17:42–45.
208. 1 Sam 18:10–11.

HONOR WITHOUT PROFIT[209]

Saul's jealousy made him quite dense
Where at first he had shown good sense.
He ought to see
From his own prophecy,
But he won't profit by the experience.

A CUT ABOVE[210]

His men an opportunity saw
To kill Saul, but David heeded law:
Trimmed the robe, then said,
"Why chase dogs that are dead?"
The king, shamed, could but hem and haw.

DEAR ABBY[211]

Against foes, David's force was a fence.
For a share of the feast they drop hints.
While trimming the wool,
Nabal's table was full.
"Your plea is just shear nonsense!"

209. 1 Sam 19:20–24.
210. 1 Sam 24:4–22.
211. 1 Sam 25:2–17.

WITCH WAY TO EXIT?[212]

Through his reign, Saul went wrong more and more;
He always kept thinking for sure
That a big sacrifice—
Not obeying—was nice.
He finally went out through the Endor.

O FAULKNER, BY GEORGE![213]

Absalom always thought that he
Was as strong as he could be.
He put on airs
About his hairs.
But he didn't—Watch out for that tree![214]

REIGN DATE[215]

If grasp of chronology you'd gain,
What co-regencies will you maintain?
New year—spring or fall?
It's a tricky call.
Reign explain is not always plain.

212. 1 Sam 15:22; 28:7–19.

213. 2 Sam 14:25–26; 18:9.

214. Cf. *George of the Jungle*. Like the site of the battle, much of Faulkner's writing is an impenetrable forest best avoided. Like Samson, Absalom brings new meaning to "bad hair day".

215. 1 and 2 Kgs.

UNSUCCESSFUL SUCCESSION[216]

Adonijah thought the crown his own,
But the choice of Solomon was soon shown.
He should have retired,
But to Abishag aspired—
Was he nursing a plot for the throne?

A BRIEF CEREMONY[217]

Which prince on the throne will sit?
David legally takes care of it:
"I solemnly swear
That Solomon goes there.
He shall be the next king"—affidavit.[218]

SOMETHING DOESN'T ADD UP[219]

In math, we know: two halves make one,
But not everything works by a sum.
Dividing a baby?
The real mom could see
As with truth, two halves will make none.

216. 1 Kgs 1:1—2:25.
217. 1 Kgs 1:28–40.
218. A pun also employed in Nash, "Ballantine", 78.
219. 1 Kgs 3:25–26.

HORSE SENSE[220]

The kingdom had begun to flower,
But stalls helped to cut short its hour.
For God did say,
"Amass horses? Nay!"
Don't trust chargers as your source of power.

TEMPLE SUBCONTRACT[221]

"Metal, clay—I must cast and fire them,
For a building fine as any in Tyre. Hmmm!
Trained slaves cost a lot,
And our craftsmen are not
As good as Phoenicians. So Hiram!"

PROVERBIAL[222]

God told Solomon, "Surely I heard.
Now faithfully obey all My word.
If you do not listen
To fulfill your mission,
From famous, you'll become a byword."[223]

220. 1 Kgs 4:26.
221. 1 Kgs 5:1–12.
222. 1 Kgs 9:2–9.
223. From lamp for the nations to lampoon.

MILITARY ESCORT?[224]

A dowry to find ere he sees her
Off—a fine gift to please her?
She should not be alone—
Who's a mature chaperone?
So Pharaoh gave to her a Gezer.

PRIDE OF PLACE[225]

Was he still on the LORD relyin',
Or was his faithfulness dyin'?
What can be known?
Based on his throne,
Solomon had crossed the lion.

FOLLOWING THE CROWD[226]

Despite Solomon's wisdom and wit,
With all his wives, he sought to fit.
What seemed a high place
In fact did abase,
Landing down in the Chemosh pit.

224. 1 Kgs 9:16.
225. 1 Kgs 10:20.
226. 1 Kgs 11:1–8.

A MINER PROBLEM[227]

Solomon's plans came a cropper
When he could no longer trade copper.
Losing mines of Edom
Showed how he did need them,
Losing the port proved to be a trade stopper.[228]

CLOAKING DEVICE[229]

By obeying, rich blessing he'd tap,
But ambition became a grave trap.
He used Ahijah's cloak
His own pride to stoke,
But he could not ever beat that wrap.

A KNICK-KNACK FOR TROUBLE?[230]

Pharaoh sought a vassal to win.
Jeroboam tried to put his own spin.
In the resulting raid
Both kingdoms paid[231]
In judgment for Solomon's sin.

227. 1 Kgs 11:14–22.

228. The revolt in Edom was thus not just a nibbling away at edges of his kingdom but a serious blow to income. Likewise, Damascus (lost around the same time) was a key crossroad for trade.

229. 1 Kgs 11:29–39; 12:25–33; 14:7–11.

230. 1 Kgs 11:26–40. This young man's skills were shown / He sought a realm of his own. / On Shishak's ally track: / "Give the man a throne! Though his old man's an unknown."

231. Although 1 Kgs 14:25–26 only mentions the attack on Judah, Pharaoh Shoshenq himself recorded extensive victories in both Israel and Judah. Perhaps Jeroboam had promised tribute and not carried through, just as he tried going his own way rather than following Ahijah's prophetic admonition to faithful obedience, or Shoshenq may have simply seen a chance to enrich himself from Solomon's riches.

VANITY[232]

Solomon in all of his glory
Taxed the people until they did worry.
So Rehoboam
Set out to show them
Who was boss, and learned in a hurry.

SCRIPTURE KNOWLEDGE PRIZE[233]

David, Solomon, Rehoboam;
In the north, start with Jeroboam,
But as for the rest,
When put to the test,
It's often confessed, "I don't know 'em."

EL[234] TURN[235]

Jeroboam and Nadab made Asherah,[236]
So God had them kicked out by Baasha.
But Baasha and son
Were not number one,
So the Baasha basher became the new pasha.[237]

---

232. 1 Kgs 12:1–18.

233. 1 Kgs 12:20–21. Such a prize was once won by Bertram Wilberforce Wooster, Wodehouse, *Life with Jeeves*, 483, 502–3.

234. El was the generic term for "god," but also used as the name of a specific deity, the father of Baal.

235. 1 Kgs 12:25–33; 14:1–20, 15:25—16:20.

236. Shrines for the eponymous consort of El, associated with warfare and fertility, equivalent to Inanna or Ishtar.

237. Not for long, though (Zimri).

DOU-BULL TROUBLE[238]

"The kingdom I'm barely done tearin'.
They might repent, and leave me barren!"
"The altar-ations I give
Are an altar-native."
As he chose to be errin' like Aaron.

NOT A BED OF ROSIES[239]

Jeroboam's thought led to a frown:
"Their center is not my own town.
I'll make my own way;
In my pocket they'll stay."
But the ashes were soon falling down.

EAT, DRINK, AND BE BURIED[240]

From the pair, oddity's evident.
But the false host knew just what it meant.
No cute figurine
Would capture this scene,
For it was not a predacious moment.

238. 1 Kgs 12:26–33.
239. 1 Kgs 13:1–10.
240. 1 Kgs 13:20–26.

NO, SIR[241]

Jeroboam's line is on the heap,
But Baasha's dynasty will not keep.
Based on the record,
He did not heed the LORD.
Thus we see that Baasha's a black sheep.

VERBAL BLAST[242]

All the kings of the north had been bad,
But Ahab was the worst that they had,
In evil complacent,
So a prophet was sent.
The word seemed a bomb of Gilead.

BAAL'S LAST STRAW[243]

They had served Baal without relent,
Yet no rain had he ever sent.
They should be aware:
Baal just wasn't there.
He merely was an Omri present.

241. 1 Kgs 15:27—16:7.
242. 1 Kgs 16:29—17:1.
243. 1 Kgs 16:29—17:1.

WHICH GOD RAINS?[244]

Baal claimed to rule the rain and thunder,
But drought made all the thoughtful wonder.
He just couldn't form
Even one little storm—
Seem's he's not over the weather, but under.

LIVE STREAMING?[245]

Israel never sought for revival,
Though sin threatened their very survival.
For grass they seek,[246]
But Baal's up the creek.
The LORD would not brook a rival.

REIGNED OUT[247]

On his home ground,[248] Baal has no grip,
No retorts to Elijah's quip,
Nor lightning bolt.
Trust Baal? You're a dolt.
Baal's nothing, not even a drip.

---

244. 1 Kgs 17:1. A common appeal of pagan gods is that they generally do less reining of morals.

245. 1 Kgs 18:5–18.

246. If he sent rain for the pastures, he could be a heavenly fodder.

247. 1 Kgs 18:19–29.

248. Besides having an established high place for Baal on it, Mount Carmel was at the border with Phoenicia. However, the brook at its base (Kishon), where the prophets of Baal were executed, was also the site of a previous example of God showing up the followers of Baal by controlling the weather. Sisera's defeat was at the Kishon, flooded by the storm that bogged down his chariots.

ALTAR-CATION[249]

Their antics could not avail.[250]
Jezebel's prophets did fail.[251]
Elijah soon bested
Then had them arrested
And charged them with jumping Baal.

NO ANSWER[252]

Trusting Baal for weather makes you sad.
Now in fighting he's equally bad.
Will the battle be won
By Baal-Hadad's son?[253]
"I need some more help here. Hey, Dad?!"

A *BIT-*[254] OF A SUCCESSION DISPUTE[255]

Two failures, success, then a siege
Which failed, then slain by his liege.
Ben-Hadad was unfit,
Hazael did his *bit-*,
But Shalmaneser was out of his league.

---

249. 1 Kgs 18:26–40.

250. His ignoring them when they gashed themselves was the unkindest cut of all.

251. Baal seemed to have bailed on them.

252. 1 Kgs 20:1–30.

253. The name Ben-Hadad, used by multiple kings of Aram, means "son of Hadad"; Baal Hadad, or "Lord Hadad" being their chief deity. Jezebel, from Tyre, would probably have used the name Baal-Melqart for her preferred version, but in general what we know of regional beliefs indicates that the two versions were quite similar.

254. *bit-*: "house of," equivalent to Hebrew *beth-*. Bit-[king] was a standard way that the Assyrians referred to other kingdoms (*e.g.*, *bit-Khumri* for Israel as the House of Omri).

255. 1 Kgs 20; 22:29–40; 2 Kgs 6:24—7:15, 8:7–15.

PLAIN FACTS[256]

A watch they ought to maintain,
Not drinking to addle the brain.
For battle ills,
They blamed the hills:
Flattery, when the problem was plain.

ESCAPE GOAT[257]

In a rematch, Ben-Hadad was bidding
Of Israel himself to be ridding.
Our narrator notes:
They seemed mere flocks of goats.
One might think that the prophet was kidding.

NO THANK YOU[258]

"Israel's known for leniency.
Will they relent? We will go and see."
Thus Aram was spared,
But Naboth? None cared.
Jezebel is *la belle dame sans merci*.[259]

256. 1 Kgs 20:23–25.
257. 1 Kgs 20:26–28.
258. 1 Kgs 20:31–33; 21:15.
259. A bit different from Keats, "Merci," 244–7.

A STRIKING MESSAGE[260]

The request did seem odd, beyond doubt,
But the Lord's orders should have had clout.
"On strike" gets a twist
As he's struck from the list.
With "no strikes" against him, he's out.

BAAL-FULL INFLUENCE[261]

"I want that land, which Naboth won't grant."
But she said "You're the king! Don't say 'can't!'"
Her background showed through:
As her niece Dido[262] knew,
Jezebel clearly was a Tyre aunt.

THIRD TIME'S THE HARM[263]

"Whatever you plan, I will do.
I am now just as one with you!"
If that were so,
Then to death he'd go,
But Aram saw that it was not true.

---

260. 1 Kgs 20:35–42.

261. 1 Kgs 21:1–16.

262. Ethbaal, king of Tyre, was Jezebel's father and the grandfather of Dido, queen of Carthage, famed for supposedly swooning over Aeneas. Carthage was getting started as a Phoenician colony around this time.

263. 1 Kgs 22:4–33.

THE CHANCE OF A LIFETIME[264]

The king thought that his plan was fab:
"My disguise will be robes that are drab!"
This hid him from man,
But not from God's plan:
A shot just at random[265] hit Ahab.

THE BIG SCREEN[266]

After tumbling down through the wall,
"Lattice pray, to Baal-Zebub we call!"
To screen out the Fly Baal
The lattice did fail,
Nor did it work to screen his fall.

I'LL FLY AWAY?[267]

God knows all that Ahaziah does:
How he flies to Baal, though he was
Taught about the LORD
Through Elijah's word,
But the "Lord of Flies" did not know the buzz.[268]

---

264. 1 Kgs 22:29–35.

265. For an illustration of a student misinterpretation of the incident, see Seuss in Abingdon, *Boners*, 39.

266. 2 Kgs 1:2.

267. 2 Kgs 1:2–6.

268. It was embarrassing, as the fly was undone.

ALL FIRED UP[269]

Ahaziah's wrath did quickly steam.
"That was surely Elijah, I deem.
He dares to despise
The Lord of the Flies?
We'll fetch him with a SWAT team."[270]

TRUTH RE-VEALED[271]

The Bethelites their calf did cherish.
Elisha—true prophet—not their dish.
A gang of youths sought to mock
And disparage his lock.
Their bull market quickly turned bearish.[272]

A SPICE OF LIFE[273]

The stew was nicely piping hot,
Then they saw there was death in the pot.
By direct a salt,
He mended the fault.
Thus Elisha cut the gourdian not.

269. 2 Kgs 1:9–12.
270. He sought to promote the fly, by knight.
271. 2 Kgs 2:23–24.
272. One way to bear your burdens.
273. 2 Kgs 4:38–41.

NOT A POT OF GOLD[274]

When Naaman had just barely gone,
Gehazi's greedy scheme then did dawn.
"You want what he had?
You'll get it, my lad."
Thus he's caught in his leper con.[275]

HEADS UP![276]

The axe couldn't cut it; instead,
It broke. "I can't repay!" he said.
It was their turn
This lesson to learn:
Trust God as the lifter of your head.

BLIND MEN'S BLUFF[277]

At leaks the Arameans were sore.
To capture Elisha they swore.
But this attack
Soon did bite back:
They'd let slip the dodges of war.[278]

---

274. 2 Kgs 5:20–27.

275. The charming goods that he took from Naaman were tragically suspicious, despite not including sugary breakfast cereal. Thus Gehazi failed his sybil service exam.

276. 2 Kgs 6:4–7; Ps. 3:3.

277. 2 Kgs 6:8–23.

278. Cf. Mark Anthony, Shakespeare, "Julius Caesar," 1120.—"let slip" is from their leashes.

UNWISE ALLIES[279]

To Israel, he showed affection,
Nearly causing his line's dereliction.
His son, Ahab's daughter . . .
Jehoshaphat ought ter
See Astarte[280] in the wrong direction.

DRIVEN TO VIOLENCE[281]

"His driving's so awful!" they yell.
"Like Jehu!" He'd been told to fell
The house of Omri
By divine decree
Because they weren't saved by the Bel.[282]

CHARIOTS OF FIRE[283]

Those who from age no wisdom did derive
But wished they were still twenty-five
Went off like a shot
To the chariot lot
And asked, "What would Jehu drive?"

---

279. 2 Kgs 8:18.

280. Astarte and Astaroth are designations for a major female deity, consort of Baal.

281. 2 Kgs 9:1–3, 9:20.

282. Bel (or Baal, or Ba'al, or Belus) was a generic term for "lord" and was applied to many deities and kings (Hadad, Melquart, Marduk, Kemosh, Molech, Zeus, and Ashur, among others). This is part of why applying the term to God tended to go along with syncretistic errors and was highly criticized by Hosea.

283. 2 Kgs 9:20.

GONE TO THE DOGS[284]

Jezebel's ethics were rather shady,
For her sins Jehu made sure she paid. He
Took over the nation
With her defenestration.[285]
She was made up, like an *aven*[286] lady.

DON'T BANK ON IT[287]

Jehu's better than some, no doubt,
But God's law he continued to flout.
He reformed by half,
For he kept the calf,
But hoped for credit from his Baal-out.

WHEN ALL ELSE FAILS, FOLLOW DIRECTIONS[288]

Water tunnel, strong walls, a whole host
Of allies: all failed. Seems he's toast.
But in his great need,
The Lord he did heed,
Knowing Sennacherib's was an idol boast.

284. 2 Kgs 9:30–37.

285. Although there's a spicy condiment called Jezebel sauce, the narrative suggests that Jezebel sauce should refer to Gravy Train.

286. *Aven* (Heb.) iniquity.

287. 2 Kgs 10:28–29.

288. 2 Kgs 18:13—19:7.

NOT SO RHETORICAL QUESTION[289]

"My king fights with power and vim!
There's no way you can stand against him!
What are the odds
You'll be saved by your gods?"
For Sennacherib, they proved very slim.

WHO PAYS FOR THE WALL?[290]

Trusting might was his first decision.
Wall and hole were built with great precision
For water supply—
Not looking on high.
For Hezekiah had tunnel vision.[291]

IT ONLY TAKES A SPARK[292]

The cults of the heathen did inspire
Human sacrifice, with gruesome pyre,
'Til Josiah did smash
And start dumping trash.
Now Gehenna[293] is a dumpster fire.

289. 2 Kgs 18:19–35; 19:37.

290. 2 Kgs 20:20; 2 Chr 32:5.

291. Although at other points Hezekiah showed faith, he fell into the error of trusting political alliances and power.

292. 2 Kgs 23:11; Mark 9:42–48.

293. The Valley of Hinnom or Gehenna in New Testament times was a burning trash heap and thus served as a name for hell.

HOW MANY KINGS DOES IT TAKE TO CHANGE A WICK?[294]

David's amazed at what God promised him,
Yet grave sin brought on judgment grim.
His lamp won't go out—
That's beyond doubt.
But often, the bulb was quite dim.

DON'T COUNT YOUR BLESSINGS BEFORE THEY HATCH[295]

Joab at the king's command winces?
It's to number the nation's defenses.
Though David knew
By many or few
God could save; take leave of your census.[296]

CENSUS AND SENSIBILITY[297]

David's theological slumber
With plague the land did encumber.
Call on God, not men,
Or troubles begin:
That's why troops had an unlisted number.

294. 1 Chr 17.
295. 1 Chr 21.
296. Cf. 1 Sam 21:13.
297. 1 Chr 21.

DINNER DIPLOMACY[298]

The queen came with her delegation,
And saw all Solomon's decoration.
They talked about prices
And trade in spices
To rank as a most flavored nation.[299]

BREAKFAST OF CHAMPIONS?[300]

For the moment, Rehoboam did learn
Not away from God's command to turn.
Stores of food and arms
Helped make towns safe from harms—
Thus fortified with vitamins and iron.

TALK OR WALK?[301]

Abijah defeated Jeroboam
When he asked the Lord to show them
Who was God. Thus in need
He spoke well, but in deed?
Too few good ones to make a poem.

---

298. 2 Chron 9:1–9.

299. Hence Eccl 3:1a: "To everything, there is a season."

300. 2 Chr 11:5–12.

301. 2 Chr 13.

OUT OF STEP[302]

Asa's victory was complete
When God's word with full trust he did meet.
But trust in Ben-Hadad?
At prophet did stay mad?
These steps led to agony of de feet.[303]

JUMPING JEHOSHAPHAT?[304]

When faced with many enemies,
Jehoshaphat got down on his knees.
As the Hebrews sang praise,
Foe killed foe in a craze.
Judah's leap of faith taken with ease.

GOOD, BAD, OR WEAK[305]

Many bad kings reigned in Judah, yet
Worse than Jehoram is hard to get.
He was such a lout,
When his bowels came out,
He died to no one's regret.[306]

---

302. 2 Chr 14–16.

303. They were *faux pas*.

304. 2 Chr 20:1–25.

305. 2 Chr 21:12–20. "Good, bad, or weak" is the classification of kings, Sellar and Yeats, *1066*, 48.

306. Perhaps Athaliah (who was also Mrs. Jehoram and Jezebel Jr.) had some regret, but the Chronicler was unlikely to think that her opinion counted.

BUY FAITH[307]

Some kings to the temple gave well,
But others to fell idols fell.
Because of these things,
In rating the kings,
One should ask, "Whose toll's for the Bel?"

POLLUTED ENVIRONMENT[308]

The lure of more power did send the
King to a disastrous end. He
Should heed Pharaoh
But instead did go
Unsustainably—not Neco-friendly.

BAD HEIR[309]

Independence by Pharaoh was clipped.
To Egypt Joahaz was shipped.
Pharaoh put in
Jehoiakim,
To be a fresh prince, of Egypt.[310]

307. 2 Chr 24:1–19; 28:22–29; 29; 33; 34:1–21.

308. 2 Chr 35:20–24.

309. 2 Chr 36:1–3.

310. Cf. the alternate title for Boyz in the Sink's version of Exodus in Roberts, *Moe*. Babylon and Egypt exerted rival prince-I-pulls, which swayed Jehoiakim and Zedekiah.

INCOME AND OUTCOME[311]

"To pursue our attack upon these
Jews, what pretext can we seize?
Claim threat to revenue!
That surely will do
To get attention from our-tax-Xerxes."

OFFICIAL RESPONSE[312]

The Jews' neighbors' schemes were nefarious,
But Tattenai wisely wrote back to Darius.
"Certainly, they should build.
Hinder them, you'll be killed."
Then all of them helped with nary a fuss.

LANDWALKER[313]

Scars of war had faded, by and by.
Ezra sought a return, then to try.
"No force need we!"
Thus we see that the
Empire sent back the return of the Levi.

311. Ezra 4:7–16.
312. Ezra 5:3–6:13.
313. Ezra 7:1—8:32.

BALD FACTS[314]

When Ezra learned of unlawful pairs,
He tore his robe, pulled out his hairs.
They acknowledged their faults,
But more lasting results
Came when Nehemiah pulled out theirs.[315]

STINGING IN THE RAIN[316]

Would the return now become just a dud?
Indictments and rain both did flood.
As the lecture advances,
Those with encumbrances
Soon knew their and the month's names were mud.[317]

POETIC JUSTICE[318]

As the rain soaked into the ground,
The law their consciences found.
Each wrongful spouse
Was in the doghouse,
Or sent to the Ezra pound.[319]

---

314. Ezra 9:1—10:4; Neh 13:25.

315. An observation going back at least to Matthew Henry.

316. Ezra 10:7–11.

317. This was the 20th of the 9th month; the 10th month, Tevet (roughly December to January), basically means "mud" in recognition of the cold and rainy weather typical for the region. The old English Solmonath (and Hobbit *Solmath*) for February meant the same. Evidently the unfaithful in the audience weren't good soil.

318. Ezra 10:7–11.

319. Having to read modern poetry might have been a worse punishment, though.

BUILDING CONSENSUS[320]

Many say, "I do not understand!
Why not let them lend a hand?"
If the plight of the Jews
To Nehemiah was news,
Who had helped to carry the firebrands?[321]

DECIMATION[322]

The people had promised to mind
Laws on giving, but later did find
Time slipping by
With nothing for Levi.
No blessed tithes left them in a bind.

WHO'S IN CHARGE?[323]

The king's order had proved a damp squib.
"If our wives hear of this, they'll be glib!"
"Ideas in the harem!"
These thoughts did scare 'em.
"All this could lead to women's lib!"

320. Neh 1:2–4; 2:19–20; Ezra 4:23.

321. The fact that Nehemiah was devastated by the news suggests that the report was not merely of unrepaired damage from the Babylonian destruction, but rather a recent attack on what had been rebuilt.

322. Neh 13:10–14.

323. Esth 1:10–22. Besides the male/female rivalry, Ahasuerus is depending on his advisors to tell him how to save face, and both the king and his advisors look foolish in telling everyone how to run their families. Although it's never explicitly mentioned in Esther, much of the point of the book is that God is actually the one in charge.

IACTA ALEA EST[324]

To assuage when his pride was stung,
Haman to his scheme gave tongue.
He'd be judge and jury
And execute in fury,[325]
But it failed, for the jury was hung.

LEGAL THRILLERS[326]

From Ahasuerus sleep was flying,
So the records he started eyeing.
He tried to review
What he needed to do
Or else to doze off while trying.

GETTING THE HANG OF IT[327]

The vizier then thought, "I'll be crowned!";
Said, "The king's honored man should go round!"
He was lifted high,
And raised to the sky,
But not with both feet on the ground.

324. Esth 5–7. "The die is cast," attributed to Julius Caesar upon crossing
the Rubicon and thus committing himself to political and military confronta-
tion (not when a barbarian threw a pot of woad at him).

325. Carroll, *Alice*, 51.

326. Esth 6:1–3.

327. Esth 6:6–11; 7:9–10.

CRACKPOT[328]

Once by all Job seemed to be prized,
Yet now by the lowest despised.
As he went to snatch
A potsherd to scratch,
He felt thoroughly ostracacized.[329]

UNJUST DESSERTS[330]

When circumstances seem distressing,
And the Lord's plan seems to keep us guessing,
It is easy
To ask, "Why me?"
While thinking that we know why in blessing.

COLD COMFORT[331]

Eliphaz's advice often would
Have been right, but for Job he should
Not assume sin
The debate to win.
Likewise Bildad and Zophar—not zo good.[332]

---

328. Job 2:8.

329. Ostracon (pl. ostraca): a pottery shard. Ostraca were widely used as scoops, scrapers, writing surfaces, *etc.* The use here shows that Job felt terra-cottable. In ancient Athens, ostraca were used for ballots in voting to expel selected politicians, hence "ostracize." Reviving that custom might have benefits.

330. Job 2:10.

331. Job 12:2.

332. As opposed to, *e.g.*, the sentiment of the psalmist in Ps 98:6 hearing the Temple trumpet: "Shofar, so good".

SKELETONS IN THE LINEN CLOSET[333]

Sorry comforters, who have no grip
On the true cause of Job's sudden slip:[334]
Blanket condemnation
Made of fiction is spun
To cover Job's case with a quilt trip.

NUGGETS OF KNOWLEDGE[335]

"There are diggings where men can get
Silver, by much skill, and yet
Wisdom can't be found
On or under ground."
Thus says Job, as a miner prophet.

CHUCK BURIED GEMS FOR WISDOM[336]

Wisdom is more precious than gold,
Much better than riches untold.
But where is it found?
Not in the ground,
Nor Columbia,[337] but Heaven, we're told.

---

333. Job 16:2–5.

334. They're not even warm.

335. Job 28.

336. Job 28:12–16.

337. Verse 14b "and the sea says, 'It is not with me.'" So wisdom is not a "gem of the ocean."

FAST AS GREASED LIGHTNING[338]

In oilier times, Job had hope,
Yet now in the dark he must grope.
Life was butter then,
But soon did begin
To prove to be a slippery slope.

FREE SPEECH[339]

Elihu thought that he could see
Flaws in the arguments of the three.
But when they heard,
"I am full of words,"
Few then and now would disagree.

PHYSICIAN, HEAL YOURSELF[340]

The most pitiable man on the globe!
In mourning, each friend tore his robe.
But in trying to diagnose,
They weren't even close.
The tables turned: they were patients of Job.

338. Job 29:6.
339. Job 32:18.
340. Job 42:7–9; Jas 5:11.

NOTEWORTHY EFFORT[341]

Much comfort the Psalms have afforded,
But the music could not be recorded.
They did not note each note
As each psalmist wrote,
So today the psalms must be rechorded.

TRUE TO LIFE?[342]

No humans do good? From the start,
This conflicts with supposedly smart
Ideas about man.
But David began
By knowing the state of his own heart.

WORKS WON'T WORK[343]

"Our wall was designed with great smarts.
It's sure to stop slingstones and darts."
"Our big sacrifice
Will make God feel nice!"
Both had a false trust in ram parts.

341. Pss 1—150.
342. Ps 14.
343. Pss 20:7; 40:6.

PULLING THE WOOL OVER OUR EYES[344]

"The Lord is my shepherd"—why, yes!
'Cause I am a wee, sweet lamb, I guess.
But real shepherds
Provide other words
Like stubborn, stupid, and helpless.

MELLOW DRAMATIC[345]

When idolaters would take fright,
God's people rejoice and delight.
A mighty tempest
With insight is blessed,
Though it was a dark and stormy night.[346]

DIS-CHORD[347]

Some claim, "Worship's going to pot!
Newfangled music? What rot!
Cello or violin
Wouldn't be sin,
But guitar?! It says here 'Fret not!'"

---

344. Ps 23.

345. Ps 29:3–9.

346. Bulwer-Lytton, *Paul Clifford*, 1, much copied by Snoopy in his efforts to be a big read dog.

347. Ps 37:1.

OH, DEER[348]

Exiled Korahite[349] felt that he
Was stag-nating in far Galilee[350]
He went beyond
Merely being fawnd
Of his God, with love that was hart-y.

FORCE OF HABIT[351]

If you don't let your pride take a hit,
Stubbornness worse and worse will get.
You'll make your will strong
If, all the day long,
You constantly exercise it.

NOT FOR LONG-BOWS[352]

Their might in archery they all tout,
But in trial, each proved a loud lout,
Not a hot shot.
When battle was fought
Ephraim's warriors soon bowed out.

---

348. Ps 42.

349. As the Psalm expresses longing for Zion in contrast to geographic features of northeastern Israel, it seems plausible that the writer had been captured in one of the Israel versus Judah confrontations.

350. The buck stopped there.

351. Ps 78:8.

352. Ps 78:9.

BEST NEST[353]

The psalmist wished the birds to follow
By staying where God's presence did hallow.
The species we know
As the *Hirundo*
rustica rustica[354]—barn again swallow.

TREADING TO HOLY GROUND[355]

Though Phoenicia often earned God's ire,
There was promise of something higher.
Her dogged persistence
Made the woman an instance
Of firstfruits of a Pneumatic Tyre.[356]

CON OR CONTEXT?[357]

Satan, wily serpent of old,
Prowls around like a lion bold.
"You're protected, surely!
Jump off so we see!"
But the next verse he left untold.

353. Ps 84:3.

354. The Eurasian subspecies of the barn swallow, which commonly builds its mud nest under eaves.

355. Ps 87:4; Mark 7:24.

356. Achieved by not having an inflated view of oneself, but rather inner tube truth.

357. Ps 91:11–13; Matt 4:6–7.

STOP SIGN[358]

From history, we should all know:
Spurning grace is not the way to go.
Consider your choice
When you hear His voice:
Going your way leads to "whoa" or "woe."

STUBBLE TROUBLE[359]

Even if you do all that you can,
You'll just be a flash in the pan.
All flesh is as grass
And will soon pass,
Self-trust relies on a straw man.

GRAVEN ERROR[360]

The idols of all the nations
Are nothing but man's creations.
Their servants become
Like them—blind, dumb.
Not gods, but statues of limitations.[361]

---

358. Ps 95:7–11.
359. Ps 103:15.
360. Ps 115:5–8.
361. The enchaining effects of idolatry create Baal bonds.

OX, HOUSE, CAMEL[362]

"A framework to say how many
Blessings in God's Word I see?
Can I tell every bit's
Delight yet make it
Easy as ג ב א can be?"[363]

BOW JEST[364]

As a parent, you will seek to know
The right time to let your arrow go.
If you have a daughter,
You learn that you oughter
Plan to send her out with a beau.[365]

SIBLING RIVALS[366]

Some like to speak of the brotherhood of man.
The topic's old—with Abel it began.
Then with Jacob and Esau . . .
Thus to psalmist, he saw
Harmony as Aaron's oil that ran.

---

362. Ps 119.

363. Aleph, Beth, Gimel is Ox, House, Camel, after common words start-
ing with each letter.

364. Ps 127:4–5. Possible variations on this pun are legion, though perhaps
foreign to this setting.

365. Modernizing the metaphor would suggest that good caliber is
important.

366. Ps 133.

DONNE BE FOOLED[367]

Beauty has many valid roles,
But it lures fools into dark holes.
Do not assume
That you are immune:
Ask not for whom the belle trolls.

ANT-ICS[368]

A sluggard who feels his lacks,
To an anthill should duly make tracks.
You'll see what is meant,
For they are diligent.
If he learns, that's an anty climax.

ROADS SCHOLAR[369]

In the crossroads and squares, Wisdom cries.
With her rival of Folly she vies,
Not just for the elite,
But for any who meet
Her, they can learn to be street wise.

367. Prov 5.
368. Prov 6:6–8.
369. Prov 8–9.

DOWN PAYMENT[370]

To seek our own way we conspire,
In pride we strive to get higher.
Thinking we're tall
Leads to a fall,
And keeps us all down in the mire.

FIELD OF DREAMS[371]

In his land all but weeds are now dead.
To excuse this, the sluggard has said:
"There might be a lion![372]
Going out would mean dyin'!"
So he's manely lyin' in bed.

A SECOND OPINION[373]

Seek and heed criticism so that
You grow wise—do not merely chat.
Iron sharpens iron,
From good critiques I learn.
A lone iron just makes things flat.[374]

---

370. Prov 16:18.
371. Prov 24:30–31; 26:13.
372. The thought gives him paws.
373. Prov 27:17.
374. Those nearby may even get steamed. Thus, flattery gets you nowhere.

WELL-INSURED[375]

The small may yet find a way
To be wise, and thus win the day.
The gecko who crawls
Upon the king's walls
Might be imperial Tokay.[376]

KEEPING IN STITCHES[377]

Her family has tranquility,
For her skills have great utility.
His wife's praise he sings:
"She makes many things,
For she has much flax ability."[378]

PLUMBING THE PSYCHE[379]

To shine a bright light so we see
That reliance on what is physically
Evident will sink
Us to the brink
Of despair, the Preacher pipes up "Vanity!"[380]

---

375. Prov 30:24–28.

376. One common gecko species is named for its "to-kay" call, as if requesting the Hungarian wine Imperial Tokay, cited by Doyle, "Sign of Four", 156; Sayers, "Bibulous", 165.

377. Prov 31:10–31.

378. Thus, having the household well-clothed for winter might be the first health care flax plan. It had good coverage.

379. Eccl 1:2.

380. Perhaps Solomon concluded "All is vanity" after getting the bill from Hiram for harem bathroom fixtures, even though Solomon was flush with cash.

PITIFUL PARTY (-ERS) [381]

Folly won't get you in the pink;
Nor will it help you to think.
'Tis no good to party,
Everything's vanity
On the earth; even the kitchen sink.

NO OUTLET [382]

Much of life does not look pretty
With no light with which we can see.
Life seen at large
Gave him no charge;
The Preacher saw eclectic futility. [383]

VAIN THOUGHTS [384]

Solomon tried having fun
With everything under the sun,
But without the LORD,
He quickly got bored,
For all had already been done.

381. Eccl 1:2; 2:12–17.
382. Eccl 1:2.
383. It should shock us out of complacency.
384. Eccl 1–3.

90

HALF SHARE[385]

"Though I work with my great wisdom,
Who knows what will after me come?"
The sad truth is
Only he was the whiz;
Rehoboam was merely dumb.

LET THE CIRCLE BE BROKEN[386]

If your attitude is one of doubt,
Each day's a Sisyphus-like bout.
In this round times table,[387]
No person is able
To find corners in which to take time outs.

SHARPENING OLD SAWS[388]

Qoheleth, in his teaching role,
Collected sayings and made a whole.
That which could be penned
Never comes to an end,
But some books are merrisome to the soul.

---

385. Eccl 2:19–20.

386. Eccl 3:1–8.

387. The sources of tedium multiply. A cyclical view of history, though popular at various times (*e.g.*, among "Enlightenment" deists), tends towards pessimism, in contrast to the biblical picture of history having a direction and meaning.

388. Eccl 12:9–12.

GRADING ON THE CURVE[389]

She thinks his the best of all faces;
They can't get enough of embraces.
He has no reserves
For he's sure that the curves
Have fallen to him in pleasant places.[390]

CORE VALUES[391]

He's as pleasant as if he had plied her
With apples. To the shade he'll guide her.
She's sure that this guy
Is her sweetie-pie.
She wants him to always be cider.[392]

BETTER TO HAVE LOVED AND FLOSSED[393]

"Your teeth match!" shows that he is happy.
"Like ewes and lambs with no mishap!" She
Can give a wide grin
Without letting light in!
True love, for her smile is a-gap-y.

389. Song 1—8; Ps 16:6.

390. Statisticians tell us this is a normal response to belle curves.

391. Song 2:3.

392. The fruitful metaphor is quite ap-peeling for puns, but the mushiness of sentiment might make others think of applesauce.

393. Song 4:2.

WELL-LIKED[394]

In gushing on a prospective mate,
Of similes there's quite a spate.
"Legs like carved stone,"—for thus
She says, "He's marble-ous;"
"Like a palm tree,"—he hopes for a date.

LAST AID[395]

Their neighbors' ways she did ape;
Judah's health will too quickly escape.
As her own way she goes,
She rots head to toes.
Never fear—she has rolls of duct tape.

OUT, SPOT![396]

Empty rite on the LORD grates;
Injustice and evil He hates.
Turn and repent,
Then cleansing is sent.
But refusal leaves you in dyer straits.

394. Song 5:13a; 7:7a.
395. Isa 1:4–6.
396. Isa 1:11–20.

WHOSE SON?[397]

"Ruled by children" a curse? That seems odd,
For Jesus used a child as a mod-
el for us,
But do not fuss:
A good ruler is like a child of God.

TIME FOR A BRAKE[398]

Ahaz thought that his idolatry
Would make getting his way quite easy.
So he did decline
To ask God for a sign,[399]
For it would read S-T-O-P.[400]

SWIFT JUDGMENT[401]

Some things just cannot be hid
Though one tries to be of them rid.
With a name such as
Maher-shahal-hash-baz,
All knew he was a prophet's kid.

397. Isa 3:4; Mark 9:36–37.

398. Isa 7:11.

399. The sign given anyway, a virgin having a son, showed that Ahaz's idea of relying on Assyria rather than God was a miss conception.

400. Or, rather, though it doesn't rhyme as well עמד.

401. Isa 8:3.

VIA MIDIAN[402]

Rule by force shall one day expire.
The soldiers will all retire.
Military gear
Shall disappear:
It's all burnt in the boot campfire.

BALK LIKE AN EGYPTIAN?[403]

"From Assyria we now can revolt,
For Egypt says 'To your side I'll bolt!'"
But when battle came near,
No help did appear.
Trust in Egypt shows that you are a dolt.

JUST IN CASEMATE[404]

Nice exteriors can hide all
The trash piled inside a wall.
The more we indulge,
And don't heed the bulge,
The greater will be our fall.[405]

---

402. Isa 9:3–5.

403. Isa 30:1–7.

404. Isa 30:13. Casemate walls are built from two narrow, parallel walls. The space in between is then reinforced by dumping in dirt or whatever junk is handy. This is a much easier way to build a thick wall than to make one solid, massive wall. However, flaws in the walls can allow the filling to push down and outwards. A casemate wall with a bulge is about to collapse catastrophically.

405. A pattern observed in diet as well as in morals.

CRASH AND BURN[406]

Israel's deeds have ruined their lot:
Their dead unburied—they'll sit and rot.
Breaking their covenants
Will bring punishments:
Being cheatos, they'll be flamin' hot.[407]

LEARN OR BURN[408]

Trust in what's man-made will one day fall.
Our folly should surely appall:
It's theological slumber
To be fooled by lumber.
Such a god wooden't help you at all.[409]

A BIG SHOW[410]

The idols are of no avail.
Even just to roll along, they fail.
Pagans say something
Yet they know nothing,
For they must always tote that Baal.

406. Isaiah 33:10–14; 34.

407. Daniel 3 shows that being Exxxxxxxtra Flamin' Hot is possible for the righteous as well.

408. Isa 44:9–20.

409. God's superiority to the constructed idols shows that His ways are above board, and the puns are over board.

410. Isa 46:1–2.

RAISING EXPECTATIONS[411]

The LORD alone is God Most High,
But on earth, judging solely by eye,
Many did stumble
At appearance humble,
High and lifted up—for to die.

TEMPT BREEDS FAMILIARITY[412]

We claim to have been led astray:
"To bad influence, we're helpless prey!"
But we aren't needing
External mis-leading:
We're misled when we lead the way.

I OWE, I OWE[413]

We can strive with great vigor and vim,
But our balance will still look grim.
Relief from our debt
We will not get
'Til we learn to solely lien on Him.

411. Isa 52:13–15.
412. Isa 53:6.
413. Isa 55:1–2.

OVER THE HUMP[414]

"Covered with camels" is not your thing?
"Rich blessings" has a more modern ring?
God promises many
Blessings, although He
Knows how much we are unpromising.

APORKALYPSE NOW[415]

They thought, "We will not pay a price
For hiding in the night, with the mice.
God will not see
These things done by me;
He will not watch My Hammy Vice."

OH BOIL[416]

His fellow Judeans all thought
That all that they needed, they had got.
But a warning vision
Revealed God's decision:
He saw that they'd soon go to pot.[417]

---

414. Isa 60:6.
415. Isa 65:2–7.
416. Jer 1:13–16.
417. Trouble was brewing.

DROPPED CALL[418]

God on Israel's history enlarges:
Not a straight path—well off the marges,
Quickly less noble.
Though they were less mobile,
In Canaan they faced roaming charges.

BEG FOR MERCY[419]

Ils n'ont même pas la sagesse d'un chien,
Car ils n'apprennent jamais rien.
Si on écoute,
On n'aura pas de chute,
Mais ils ne savent pas faire le bien.[420]

TURN OR BURN[421]

Judah spurned the prophets sent to mend her,
Thus into exile God will now send her.
Cashing in on each deed
Increases furnace feed.
The verdict: they're legal tinder.

---

418. Jer 2:1–8.

419. Jer 4:22.

420. They don't even have the wisdom of a dog, For they never learn anything. If one listens, one won't fall, but they don't know how to do what is good. "*Faire le bien*"—do what is good; "*faire le bon*" literally, do the good, but is the French idiom for telling your dog to sit up and beg.

421. Jer 5:1–14.

FALLEN SPRING[422]

Stern warnings Jeremiah did tell,
But the message just wouldn't sell.
Nobody heeds reason:
"The prophets artesian!"
Everyone is a ne'er do well.

PROPHETS TO FIT[423]

To listen to truth they declined.
Soothing prophets were easy to find.
Rather than warn,
They'd blow their own horn,
Giving people a peace of their mind.

PEACE [IS] OUT[424]

Saying "Peace!" does not help at all,
For Judah is destined to fall.
They sin all the day.
Ashamed? There's no way.
They're so far past any recall.

422. Jer 6:7.
423. Jer 6:10–14.
424. Jer 6:14–15.

NO SILVER METAL[425]

Like bad ore, mined in vein, futilely:
Refining produces dross only.
Therefore, the LORD thinks
That their repentance stinks,
For all of the people smelt badly.

TRUST BUSTING[426]

The popular mantra was simple:
"The temple, the temple, the temple!"
But God didn't delight
In rite without right.
False trust bursts like a big pimple.

PROOF TEXT[427]

The temple ought to show forth God's name,
But their greed made it a grievous shame—
Through their brazen sin,
A robbers' den.
Here's one verse health and wealth folks can claim.

425. Jer 6:27–30.
426. Jer 7:4–15.
427. Jer 7:11.

THE COST OF CHEAP THRILLS[428]

Jeremiah's warnings were hated,
For obeying God's laws just seemed dated.
Doing their own thing
Seemed exhilarating,
But it made them exile-rated.

POPULATION DENSITY[429]

The people were being quite dense,
So God gave them just recompense.
Lots of deceiving,
Not rightly believing,
And not nearly enough horse sense.

SORTING THE FOLD[430]

From Judah most folks God will cleave:
For sin, from their homes God will heave.
Your lies are your bane:
Quite few will remain,
Only those who pass through de sieve.

428. Jer 8.
429. Jer 8:16–17; 9:3–6.
430. Jer 9:5–7; 9:21.

IT'S NOT OK[431]

Jeremiah gave them solemn warning,
A call for great lament, not for scorning:
"Standard response fails—
Find a princess of wails,
It won't be a beautiful mourning."[432]

SOURED RELATIONSHIP[433]

The people were foolishly fickle.
Idols are all dead, not quick; still,
Like scarecrow 'midst cucumbers.
Zero's all their numbers.
They will just leave you in a pickle.[434]

WRONGFUL IN-TENT[435]

My sins made my tent history.
I miss stakes—sons pegged out on me.
At the end of my rope,
There is no hope.
Dis-cord means curtains for drapery.

431. Jer 9:17–19.
432. Everything was going away.
433. Jer 10:1–16.
434. Showing that idols are a vine hope.
435. Jer 10:20.

VEGGING OUT[436]

"Why are schemers planted by you?
The evil wreak vengeance anew."
"Planted? Six feet under!
At them, do not wonder.
They reek of Baal worship: they're through."

BELTED OUT[437]

The Lord does not judge in haste,
But obedience was not to their taste.
All of the band
Was out of hand.
Clearly they had gone to waist.

PLANNING GROWTH[438]

"I gave them no root nor a stem!
'No famine or battle,' say them!"
The people were fans
Of grand, false plans.
Deceit's de seat of de problem.

436. Jer 11:16–24; 12:1–2.
437. Jer 13:1–11.
438. Jer 14:13–16.

DATA IN THE CLOUD[439]

Though there's use in the natural laws,
Trusting only them leads to grave flaws;
Idols vanish like mist—
Baal's no meteorologist;
We need a clear view of ultimate cause.

A PROPHET WITHOUT HONOR[440]

Neither a borrower, nor a lender me,
Yet all that I meet is hostility.
They refuse to get
That we're so deep in debt
We must trust in grace that is free.

NOT-SO-INTERMITTENT FASTING[441]

The souls of Judeans weren't beaming,
However, their idols were all gleaming.
They'll starve on the earth
Due to their faith's dearth.
The invaders will fast be teeming.

439. Jer 14:22.
440. Jer 15:10.
441. Jer 16:1–13; 17:1–4, 12–13.

DON'T MEET AT THE POLE[442]

"How could God think to call me a sinner?"
You're always stretching His patience thinner.
It's near the last lap,
And idols are a trap.
In the pole position is no winner.

IN THE GROOVE[443]

Apostasy the people did catch
So them to exile foes will soon fetch.
What each did engrave
Will make him a slave,
Until God shakes up the etch-a-wretch.

READY FOR THE FINAL TRUMP[444]

To us the ways that we have made
Seem right, but we have disobeyed
When it seemed to suit.
To turn us from that route,
Jeremiah called the heart a spade.

442. Jer 16:10–13; 17:2. A standard symbol of Asherah, fertility goddess
and consort of El, was a wooden pole.

443. Jer 17:1–4.

444. Jer 17:9.

NOT JUST FEET OF CLAY[445]

Would the pot be good, or a dud?
Of flaws, there seems to be a flood.
Resisting the potter
Will not hold water;
Disobeying makes your name mud.

BURNING PASSIONS[446]

The sinners were stubborn and mulish
In selfishness and every cruel wish.
We must repent and learn
Towards the Lord to turn.
To stay in our own ways is fuelish.

A BONDING EXPERIENCE[447]

No chance for deliverance, 'twas sure
If Judah showed no repentance. Her
Destruction loomed near
If she refused to hear.
All Pashhur could give was a stock answer.[448]

---

445. Jer 18:1–12.

446. Jer 18:12.

447. Jer 19:1—20:6.

448. The return on his investment in stocks and bonds was no return.

THE CASE OF THE BURNING SCROLL[449]

"The king's a case, openly wants me shut.
So my crying out, I tried to stop, but
The word of God's ire
In my bones is fire.
Though of slanders of me, there's a glut."

MORE THAN SPARE CHANGE[450]

Might God change His message abruptly,
Though all from repentance stayed free?
They expected cheap grace
To deliver that place,
But found that presumption was costly.

WHO HOLDS THE CONTROLS?[451]

Jehoiakim to grandeur did cling,
But it was just broken cisterns with bling.
He shouldn't act dumber
Than a common plumber;
Aping power made him Donkey King.

449. Jer 20:7–12.
450. Jer 21:1–12.
451. Jer 22:13–19.

MAKING AN ASS OF ONESELF[452]

Eliakim[453] just cares for gain:
His arrogance will be his bane.
He is such a creep
He'll be tossed in a heap.
The kingdom will be in great pain.

RINGLEADER[454]

"Surely our king never will fall!"
He'll be cast out, with no recall.
Thus the whole band
Is lost, off hand.
He's one ring to fool them all.

NOT LIVING UP TO THE NAME[455]

Jeremiah told of the Messiah,
Wise and just, a name will inspire:
"The LORD," we confess,
"Is our righteousness"—
In Hebrew, that's "Zedekiah."

---

452. Jer 22:11–23. An attempt to drop barrels on Jeremiah whilst he was in the cistern would have added further to being like a donkey.

453. Original Hebrew name of Jehoiakim.

454. Jer 22:24–28.

455. Jer 23:5–6.

TAXING CLAIMS[456]

A soothing word! Like Esau's broth, it
Went down well, but God said, "Get off it!"
Unless it comes true,
Your net worth is through—
You clearly are just a non-prophet."

FIGGY OFFPUTTING[457]

Good figs: exiles blessed in their station,
But bad fruit was the rest of the nation,
The prophet could see
Their security
Was a figment of the imagination.[458]

LOST IN TRANSMISSION[459]

Away from God Israel did drift.
The prophets could not heal the rift.
Beyond a doubt,
God would drive them out:
They're stuck in idol and won't shift.[460]

---

456. Jer 23:9–40.

457. Jer 24.

458. A fig Newton* would have emphasized the gravity of the situation.

459. Jer 25:3–11.

460. God provided the manual, but their apostasy seemed automatic.

TRAITORS LOSING THE ARK[461]

The message from the LORD was simple:
"Turn at once from your ways so sinful!"
An audience unequal
To Shiloh's sequel:
Jeremiah and the doom of the temple.

UNEQUALLY YOKED[462]

Jeremiah warned of Babylon's vim.
But egged on by the Judeans' vain whim,
Hananiah broke
Jeremiah's yoke.
The Jews soon found the yokes on them.

PAYING THE FIELD[463]

As Judah quickly neared her fate,
For buying, the time seemed too late.
Jeremiah did feel
That the deal seemed unreal,
God assured him it was quite real estate.

---

461. Jer 26:1–6.
462. Jer 27–28.
463. Jer 32.

IM-PATRICKAL[464]

Under siege, each master loudly sayeth:
"We free our slaves." But 'twas merely breath!
Prompt promise scorning
Prompted a warning:
"Give them liberty, or give yourselves death!"

THE PEN IS MIGHTIER[465]

Jehoiakim thought he'd heard enough,
But his deed just made his fate rough.
Writing a new scroll
Might take a toll,
But Baruch proved to have the write stuff.

JUGGED[466]

The warnings Jehoiakim did burn;
Zedekiah vacillated in turn.
Jeremiah tried
To halt Judah's slide,
But "brethren" threw him in the "cisteren."[467]

---

464. Jer 34:8–22.

465. Jer 36:20–32.

466. Jer 36:23; 34:1–22; 38:1–9.

467. Particularly ironic given Jeremiah's warning about broken cisterns back in 2:13.

WASHOUT[468]

Judeans do not change at all.
Still evil, their leaders appall.
Both wishy-washy king,
And persistent washing,
God did wash his hands of them all.

DON'T SLEEP TONIGHT[469]

Babylon felt safe in her own might,
But now sinks into the dim twilight,
By self-trust they bungle;
From the mighty jungle,
Jordan jungle, the lion seeks a fight.[470]

CALLED[471]

The reluctant prophet Jeremiah
Wished that he could retire
Off to a farm
Away from all harm,
But instead he became the town crier.

---

468. Jer 37:21; 38:4–5; Matt 23:25–26.

469. Jer 50:43–46.

470. Not just over copyright, either. ("The Lion Sleeps Tonight" is not a traditional African song, but a traditional-style song composed by an African singer who wasn't getting royalties from U.S. recordings for decades.)

471. Lam 1:1.

CHEWS THIS DAY[472]

To repent, the people long disdained,
Until they were grievously pained.
The change of heart
Has a rocky start,
But nothing dentured, nothing gained.

AN ERIE SITUATION?[473]

Grim prophecies leave him no pal;
No mourning when he's lost his gal.
Exile will be long
As you learn from the song:
Forty years on the Chebar Canal.

TIME TO LISTEN[474]

The Judeans thought that they were top-notch,
Yet mixed pagan dregs in a hotchpotch.
"Son of man, give warning.
Many will be scorning,
But for some, yours will be a stop watch."

472. Lam 3:16.
473. Ezek 1:3; 2:6–8; 4:6; 24:15–27.
474. Ezek 3:17–21.

IRON-Y[475]

The overall meaning is right at hand:
Jerusalem in the siege will not stand.
But why a griddle?
We can solve the riddle:
God reviewed them and they were panned.[476]

VALUES UNDER SIEGE[477]

From the faithless, each false trust God rips
Away: water's doled out by drips;
Food and wall give way;
Yet in revolt they stay,
Until they've cashed in all their chips.[478]

RED LIGHT TO THE NATIONS[479]

Sowing God's word among nations her duty,
But Israel bore other fruit, for she
Sought to be like the others
And get herself lovers—
Forever a goy[480] and a beauty.

---

475. Ezek 4:3.

476. The differences couldn't just be ironed out.

477. Ezek 4:1–17.

478. Or at least those of their cows.

479. Ezek 16.

480. Yiddish, from *gôy* (Heb.): gentile.

PURPLE PROSE[481]

The great ship with wealth piles higher,
To her trade all nations aspire.
But dye from murex[482]
Will not prevent wrecks.
She'll sink and never re-Tyre.

NO DIPLOMATIC HERD IMMUNITY[483]

The task of true leaders is to keep.
But if just for themselves they reap,
It's a terrible fate,
For the sheep of state
Will soon wreck if it's partisan-sheep.

A SKELETON KEY[484]

Judah had been through God's wrath;
Dead and dried—a zero by their math.
But God can restore
Displaced bones galore.[485]
Trust Him—take the osteo path.

---

481. Ezek 27.

482. The family of snails producing the purple dye used by the Phoenicians (and others). People in Lydia eventually discovered a plant that could produce the same color, hence the fortune of Lydia in Acts 16:14.

483. Ezek 34:17–22.

484. Ezek 37:1–14.

485. What seemed barren, God made into a bone-anza.

BREAK WITH TRADITION[486]

The Lord will keep all his forever,
But first, through exile they must weather.
Judah and Israel
Will not quarrel, but gel,
And finally learn to stick together.

VANITY FARE[487]

Daniel and friends did not fail
To obey God; by plain food kept hale.
They grew more strong and wise
Than the ham-and-cheese guys
And created the first veggie tale.[488]

GOLDEN LOCKS AND RUSTY TOES[489]

Humanity progresses, it is said.
But reality should strike that claim dead.
Through time we move,
Yet we don't improve.
We don't quit when we are a head.

486. Ezek 37:16–20.

487. Dan 1.

488. Later Nebuchadnezzar himself followed their example of a vegetarian diet.

489. Dan 2:31–45.

FINDING THE PATH[490]

Exile's path seemed unclear night and noon,
But the three had to find their way soon.
Interpreting a dream
Established their team,
Led by granting of a Daniel boon.

A TOUGH GRILLING[491]

The clamorous music had just begun,
When jealous folks to the king did run,
His pride was at steak,
So he sought to make
These good and faithful servants well done.[492]

TREE-MEND-US MISTAKE[493]

All that Nebuchadnezzar could see:
"Everything's to the glory of me!"
But God would soon stump
Him, show he's a chump,[494]
Thus exposing his great big-o-tree.[495]

---

490. Dan 2:49.

491. Dan 3:8–18.

492. Matt 25:21. Even though Nebuchadnezzar should have known that such outstanding administrators were rare.

493. Dan 4:13–17.

494. Cf. *Car Talk*'s Stump the Chumps.

495. Despite Daniel's advice, Nebuchadnezzar woodn't repent until he learned that God's bite was stronger than his bark. Restoration was a releaf.

HEAVY WORK[496]

An angelic servant is not your
Time-serving, heedless job botcher.
When the time is right,
He will show God's light;
Until then, a patient wait watcher.[497]

SYCOPHANCY OF A THOUSAND[498]

Daniel's faithfulness they all could note,
So his foes sought the king's ego to bloat:
"Your praise rises high,
Clear up to the sky!"
Thus they flattered Darius as *mille haut*.[499]

EMPIRES STRIKE OUT[500]

After Babylon, empire's each version
Would affect the Jewish dispersion:
Medes, Greeks, Rome
Would rule their home.
(One man's Mede is another man's Persian).

496. Dan 4:13–17.

497. Apocryphal literature such as Jubilees turned "watcher" into a generally hostile class of angels, but here it seems to merely designate the patient service called for. A wait watcher might account for Nebuchadnezzar's diet.

498. Dan 6:4–9.

499. *mille haut* = "thousand high." Darius Milhaud, among many other musical works, composed the cantata "*Les miracles de la foi*" on texts from Daniel. The "Symphony of a Thousand," however, is Mahler's.

500. Dan 7:1–8.

OUT OF SHAPE FOR THE MARATHON[501]

"The mightiest of creatures I am!"
That claim was soon proved to be sham.
As Daniel did note,
He could not e-scape goat:
For he proved not to be a dodge ram.

SHAH ENOUGH[502]

"How did you, in such a short span,
Get so many conquests in your van,
And vanquish the Persians?
"See (from modern versions)
To defeat my enemy, I ran."[503]

NOTHING NEW UNDER THE SUN KING[504]

The visions will inspire the wise
To ponder upon whom he relies.
For kings, north and south,
All have a big mouth
To have room for all of the lies.

---

501. Dan 8:3–7.
502. Dan 8:5–6.
503. Those giving replies like this might be labeled smart Alex.
504. Dan 11:5–45; 7:8.

A PYLE OF TROUBLE[505]

Hosea, he married Gomer.[506]
But she proceeded to roam. Her
Sowing she did reap;
In cash came back cheap:
Fifteen shekels plus grain, three half homers.

HALF-BAKED COMMITMENT[507]

They'd been given the title of "chosen"
Yet repentance seemed totally frozen.
This foolish self-trust
Would soon go bust:
One side burnt, one goo: baker's dozin'.

DISINHERIT THE WIND[508]

They presumed that they could count upon
Promises from which duties were sawn.
"If you won't reform,
The coming storm
Will blow you all to kingdom gone."

---

505. Hos 1–3.

506. If her parents had called her "Barney Fife," maybe some of her errant tendencies could have been nipped in the bud.

507. Hos 7:8.

508. Hos 8.

WHITHER FORECAST[509]

God's word and will? Surely they knew it,
But they constantly refused to do it.
Seeding the wind
A tempest will send.
Soon they will know that they blew it.

LEAP TO FAITH?[510]

Even the most mighty lose heart:
From their path, the swarms do not depart.
Assault[511] and battery
By locusts, many,
Showed that dead faith needs a jump start.

REALLY, JOEL?[512]

As for when a locust swarm bares
The land, so the wise man prepares
For the day of the LORD,
Which the foolish adored
For they thought it not His day, but theirs.

509. Hos 8:7.

510. Joel 1.

511. From saltare, Latin "to jump".

512. Joel 1–2.

BRANCH OFFICE[513]

Instead of somebody famous,
God sent a farmer named Amos
From his sheep and his figs,
To tell Israel's bigwigs
Many things that ought to ashame us.

UDDERLY DEPRAVED[514]

Your rites? Do not even begin!
They're just an occasion for sin.
Your prayers, sadly,
Are "Me! Me! Me! Me!
For heifer and heifer, amen."

PLUMB EVIL[515]

To God's law, no one does attune,
So justice will strike them down soon.
"They grasp at fine plums,
With their nimble thumbs,
But with plumb line, I will see who to prune!"[516]

513. Amos 1–2; 7:14.
514. Amos 4:1–5.
515. Amos 7.
516. Their proud bearing will soon be druping.

BITING COMMENTS[517]

"You're a Judean agent, I know!
Now scram, far from here! Time to go!"
If Amaziah knew,
Of a place near Peru,
He'd say "Go bug them, be Amos Quito!"[518]

AN EPHAH AND A PECK[519]

They were changing their ephahs to suit,
And their shekels were big, to get loot.
And they added husk in
To lighten the bin,
Such deeds kept chaffing at their repute.[520]

RED'S NOT READY[521]

In punishment of Jacob he saw
Not warning, but gain. Hence Esau
From his summit
Will soon plummet,
Up and down reversed like a seesaw.

---

517. Amos 7:10–13.

518. That might not have kept his voice away, however, given how popular Amos in Andes was on the radio.

519. Amos 8:4–6.

520. They had more interest in profits than prophets. Given their schemes, "gross profit" would be an accurate term for these gains.

521. Obad 1.

PIGEON TOWED[522]

Like his namesake flying towards a cove,
Jonah sought far from his God to rove.
Foolish as a squab,
Avoiding his job,
But it did not work, for the dove dove.

RETURN TO SENDER[523]

To dodge God, Jonah tried to run
For the farthest place under the sun.
It was in-e-fish-ent,
For he had to repent.
When he conceded, de-baiting begun.

IS THE MOTION SECONDED?[524]

Again God called. This time, Jonah went.
But it did not accord with his bent.
Though he did preach,
He hoped not to reach,
For he was still full of re-sent-ment.

522. Jonah 1:3–15. "Jonah" means "Dove".
523. Jonah 1–2.
524. Jonah 3:1—4:1.

FISHING FOR AN ANSWER[525]

"My prophecies might profit? What frights!"
Jonah said, "I demand my rights!"
"Your judgment is failing!"
Thus Jonah was wailing,
That God had not whaled on the Ninevites.

WHERE'S LO-RUHAMAH[526] WHEN YOU NEED HER?[527]

Jonah preached; he'd learned beyond doubt
That running off would be a washout.
Much to his distress,
He was a success,
With no boudoir[528] in which to pout.

A VINE HOPE[529]

When Jonah chose to stay back
In hope of watching God's attack,
His hut did portend
Naming Daniel's friend,
For the booth was clearly a "me shack."[530]

---

525. Jonah 4:1–9.

526. Hos 1:6: "not pitied."

527. Jonah 4:2.

528. *"Bouder"* is the French verb "to pout," so a boudoir is literally a pouting room.

529. Jonah 4:5.

530. In God's (and Jeremiah's) eyes, the lavish palace built with forced labor by Jehoiakim (Jer 22:13–23) would also merit this designation.

GRAND JURY[531]

Of indictments there is such a pile
That proceedings will take quite a while.
As a witness of worth,
God chose the earth,
Showing that there will be a terres-trial.

DOWN TOWNS[532]

From Moresheth, Micah was sent
To warn all Judah to repent.
To bring out their shame,
He played on each name,
Emphasizing the sure pun-ishment.

HEDGE[533] CLIPPER[534]

The leaders should provide protection,
But they're corrupt beyond correction.
Their gross treachery
Will rebound quickly;
Their schemes form a hedge of dereliction.

531. Mic 1:2.

532. Mic 1:8–16.

533. Micah puns with several words similar to "hedge" that convey their condemnation, but, unsurprisingly, the puns don't translate well into English.

534. Mic 7:3–4.

NOVA OR *NO VA*?[535]

Nineveh's conquests had been so many,
But the once great lion's weak and skinny.
The men flee pursuit,
Abandoning the loot.
With troops vamoosed, the king's just a ninny.

NO MORE WOLF ON THE FOLD[536]

They once scattered slingstones like BBs,
But now they had best learn from Thebes.[537]
Sennacherib, Sargon,
And Pul are all gone.
Their fate should give you heebie-jeebies.

A HIND'S FORESIGHT[538]

He argued with God with great vim.
"Justice comes, though oft through means grim,
So in faith persevere."
Then, like the fleet deer,
Habakkuk learned that strong trust behooved him.

535. Nah 2:1–13. *No va* in Spanish is "no go."

536. Nah 3:8–13. Cf. Byron, "Sennacherib," 46; Nash, "Whale," 23–4.

537. Regrettably, it ought to be pronounced Theebz, rather than fitting the rhyme scheme. Thebes is the Greek name for the Egyptian city in question, called No-Amon in Hebrew; thus, to the Ninevehites' hope for safety, Nahum's answer is No.

538. Hab 1–3.

AN IN-SEINE IDEA[539]

"Your law everyone seems to toss;
Each acts as though he's his own boss!"
"I have it in hand.
They'll soon leave the land."
"By Babylon! Isn't that a net loss?"

PREACHING TO THE CHOIR[540]

Hostile nations are judged—that sounds great!
Enemies all around that we hate.
Philistia, Egypt,[541]
Moab, Ammon are stripped,
Assyria, and Judah—hey! wait!

REBUILDING RELATIONSHIPS[542]

The harvests keep on getting worse;
Your plans seem to all go off course.
Neglecting the LORD
You cannot afford:
Choose holy place or holey purse.

---

539. Hab 1:2–17.

540. Zeph 2:1—3:5.

541. "Ethiopians" (2:12) (from the modern Nubia region) briefly ruled Egypt around this time, and has too many syllables to fit in the line.

542. Hag 1:4–6.

WAIT FOR THE SHAKE[543]

Of judgment the Jews had borne the brunt.
Now retribution they did hunt.
Calm seemed to deny
Their heartfelt cry—
All seemed quiet on the mideastern affront.

IN THE FAST LANE[544]

"The temple's built—is our fasting done?"
"Well, has any repentance begun?
You cannot fool Me
With mere self-pity.
Live justly; you can't pull a fast one."

A-MAIZING EISEGESIS[545]

"Corn shall make the young men cheerful
And new wine the maidens":[546] I'm fearful
Of thoughts of corn whiskey.
Deal with misreadings briskly:
Read this book, of corn get an earful.

---

543. Hag 2:6–7; Zech 1:10–17.

544. Zech 7:3–10.

545. Zech 9:17b.

546. KJV. Of course, in modern English, "corn" is "grain," *i.e.* good harvests under the Messianic ruler is what is actually meant. Distillation was not yet invented; no doubt corny humor had been invented, but the term wasn't.

RUSTY OBEY[547]

Steal from God—how could that be?
Malachi's not talking to me.
My tithe? What a pain!
Give the sheep with a sprain,
While I chase a heathen honey.

SCRUBBING IDEAS[548]

The Lord's messenger will soon be sent.
Let all consider the prophet's hint.
If you take the chance
For repentance,
He serves as a deter gent.

547. Mal 1–2.
548. Mal 3:1–2.

NEW TESTAMENT

GO, LOOK, AND LISTEN[1]

"Magi? A new king? That's quite rummy!"
"Check it out? Nah, my schedule's too crummy."
By being busy,
Not going to see,
Each proved to be a crèche test dummy.

GOING BOLDLY[2]

The magi their observations check
With their best astronomical tech.
They were quite wise
In this enterprise,
For they knew that it was a star trek.[3]

---

1. Matt 2:1–3; 12:42.
2. Matt 2:1–12.
3. The event later led to the founding of the kirk.

PROPHETIBLE DIET[4]

He lived off of the land he lived on;
Far from markets and fields he had gone.
Locusts and honey
To us sound funny,
Yet some still like to eat hoppin' John.[5]

FISH AND GAME?[6]

Listening may have merely seemed nice,
But now, a command, not advice:
"Don't toy with old ways,
Follow Me all your days,
Leave boats and net, that is the fisher price."

A WORD IN SEASON[7]

If we stray from God's way and waver, we
Lose all our preservative flavor. The
Chalky,[8] dull gunk
Is cast out as junk,
For our character has become unsavory.

---

4. Matt 3:4.

5. Standard recipes for this dish do not contain insects, however.

6. Matt 4:18–22.

7. Matt 5:13.

8. Natural rock salt has varying proportions of halite (table salt), calcite (chalk rock, limestone, *etc.*), and gypsum (plaster, commercial blackboard chalk), among other minerals. Halite dominates sea salt, but also dissolves easily, potentially leaving behind the unpalatable components.

UPTOWN LIFE[9]

A hilltop is a strategic sell;
Old bricks and junk pile up as well.
Thus soon is found
A town on a mound,
Not hidden—clearly show and tel(l).[10]

SI VEL NON[11]

With the straightforward truth, we must go;
Excuses and loopholes will grow.
Given our capacity
For verbal opacity,
More than a "no" becomes a no-no.

FAST AND LOOSE[12]

In the law's letter, they were well-versed,
But for godliness they did not thirst.
When they forego,
It's just for show.
Thus we see that their fast shall be worst.

9. Matt 5:14.

10. Both spellings are used for the mound built up over time on long-occupied city sites.

11. Matt 5:37, in contrast to Abelard.

12. Matt 6:16.

A SWELL IDEA[13]

"Wine to store? Why don't you fetch
Those old wineskins?" No, there's a catch.
The wine is brand new,
Old skins will not do.
The fresh wine is too much of a stretch.

SHORT CUT[14]

"I bring not peace, but a sword," is said when
The twelve's mission is all set to begin.
That does not license harm
Nor a physical arm:
You should not be fissurers of men!

YOKING AROUND[15]

"Take My yoke," calls: "Come along and pull!"
As of learning we become more full.
Being joined in
Turns us from sin.
Thus He speaks to us in pair of bulls.[16]

13. Matt 9:17.

14. Matt 10:34; 26:51–52.

15. Matt 11:29–30; Mark 4:2.

16. Not, however, the way Jereboam I claimed that He did. As the stories
can help us to reflect and focus, they serve as parabolic mirrors.

TOO SLOW A CLIP[17]

"Our laws by true rabbis are known!"
But in fact their own error was shown:
On their own rules so keen,
That God's law was not seen.
Their hedge 'round the law was overgrown.

MENDING WAYS?[18]

By their discord, evildoers are hit;
Satan tries to keep his realm well-knit.
If not for this role, he
Might see things get hole-y,
So he must always be darning it.[19]

DUN WE NOW[20]

Set free, you try to look your best.
But the evil has not gone to rest.
If you still owe,
Your fate you can know:
If not paid for, you'll be repossessed.

17. Matt 12:1–8.
18. Matt 12:25–26.
19. Such efforts are costly—it's a purl of great price.
20. Matt 12:43–45.

THE PATH OF MOST RESISTANCE[21]

"It's for the birds," some say, fruitlessly.
Others spring up, but only briefly.
For growth that will last,
The plant must hold fast
To rich soil with the Root of Jesse.

WEEDY OR NOT?[22]

A first hearing with joy we anoint,
But hearing and deeds must be joint.
Unchecked growth of weeds
Will not yield good deeds:
All the thorns make us miss the point.

SEEDY CHARACTERS[23]

When teachings just bounce off the herds,
Or worldly cares choke out God's words,
Or out comes the sun,
The words of the Son
Are then said to be for the birds.[24]

21. Matt 13:3–23.

22. Matt 13:3–23.

23. Matt 13:3–9; 18–23.

24. Tweets do seem to be a productive source for views lacking in depth.

FINAL ROUNDUP[25]

Life's garden with weeds is oft full;
Why not just give them all a pull?
Though roots of weeds
Tangle with the good seeds',
The weeds' fate is tare[26]-ible.

GOOD THINGS COME IN SMALL PACKETS[27]

Ingrained doubts often make us dismiss
Small seeds. But with force mustered, this
Grows with great relish.
What seemed just a wish
Surely will ketchup with the promise.

PUPPY LOVE[28]

She kept hounding them for assistance,
Yet Jesus seemed to just keep His distance.
His words seemed cynical,[29]
But that proved imical
To showing faith through dogged persistence.[30]

---

25. Matt 13:24–30.

26. They are weighed and found wanting.

27. Matt 13:31–32.

28. Matt 15:22–28.

29. Cynic means dog-like, probably intended disparagingly of their biting comments. This Syrophoenician woman made a much more positive association with canids than a previous Syrophoenician woman, Jezebel.

30. She'd accept just a doggie bag.

DON'T ROCK THE BOAT[31]

Simon was not ready to own
The name "Peter," 'til his faith had grown.
It took some more shocks[32]
To gain strength of rocks—
On the lake, he sank like a stone.

DIRECT(ED) PATH[33]

As grains must die[34] when they are sowed,
Under the world's weight, he'll be bowed.
The way was narrowing,
Soon to be harrowing:
The straight route proved to be the cross road.

NET PROFIT?[35]

To seem right Peter was in a rush,
But Jesus knew it not worth the fuss:
"A king tax his son?
It just isn't done.
But I know a fish with the cash for us."

31. Matt 16:15–18; 14:28–31.

32. The announcement in 16:1 of heading to the crucifixion certainly rocked Peter's world.

33. Matt 16:21–25.

34. John 12:24. Of course, botanically not all of a seed dies, but the component of the seed that is tissue from the parent plant does die.

35. Matt 17:24–27.

NOT A BULLDOZER[36]

Faith can move mountains easily,
But that does not mean that my whims are free:
Not landscaping—
It's reshaping
The human world, and especially me.

A SHOW OF FAITH[37]

Do not be like the hypocrite—
In the place of honor he'd sit.
His phylactery
Is as big as could be,
Not for God, but for fringe benefit.

A SEASONED RESPONSE[38]

You should tithe of your spice, that is true,
But with such mere externals, you're not through.
Of your mint, give the dime,
And give of your thyme,
To truly be a tarragon of virtue.

36. Matt 21:21–22.
37. Matt 23:5–6.
38. Matt 23:23.

CAMEL'S SOUP[39]

If we fuss about gnats or a beetle,
Yet not give our camels heed, we'll
Build hypocrisy.
To filter both, we
Must be squeezed through the eye of the needle.[40]

WIPE OUT[41]

Over time, their approach became hyper-
Legalism; wisdom got no riper.
They only would clean
The part that is seen:
No vonder that He called them vipers.

WHITEWASH WASHOUT[42]

When on our good deeds we make our stance,
We have not got a ghost of a chance.
A coat of whitewash
Is just so much bosh—
No hope comes from that repaintance.

---

39. Matt 23:24.
40. Curiously, squeezing through the eye helps us to get the point.
41. Matt 23:25–26, 33.
42. Matt 23:27–28.

POOR LITTLE RICHARD GIRLS[43]

The lamps were all wick-ed, I surmise—
It took being fuelish to be wise.
Whether the five got
Health and wealth, or not,
They were oily to bed, oily to rise.

CROSS PURPOSES[44]

The Sanhedrin thought that they were all
Rid of Jesus, killed outside the wall.
But then a big rip
Would give folks a tip
That He'd soon make a curtain call.

A BIG LETDOWN[45]

In their paralytic friend's distress,
They trust Jesus, but then face a mess,
From media clout,
Liberal, no doubt:
They could not reach Him, "because of the press."[46]

43. Matt 25:1–13. Not olive them were ready.
44. Matt 27:51.
45. Mark 2:4.
46. KJV. There was no in in the room.

STAND UP FOR JESUS[47]

The Pharisees think themselves wise,
Yet miss what's before their own eyes,
Not learning as they ought.
Because they sought
To lay down law, they cannot say, "Arise!"

INFERNAL REVENUE SERVICE[48]

"Don't you know that everyone sees
That no rabbi would hang out with these?
Your teacher should beware!
He won't get anywhere
If he hails taxers instead of taxees!"

A STITCH IN TIMES PAST[49]

Patching's usefulness will soon decrease;
Trying to mend must finally cease.
Attempting to stitch
When it's time to switch
Is saying "Piece, Piece," when there is no piece.

---

47. Mark 2:6–11.
48. Mark 2:16.
49. Mark 2:21.

DONNER AND BLITZEN[50]

They lacked control, like unbroken colts.
Zeal without knowledge to judgment bolts.
It is no wonder
They are "sons of thunder":
Not learning made them be thunderdolts.

WHO'S OUT OF THEIR MIND?[51]

Their malice was in evidence,
For the claim was not merely dense,
But beyond belief!
With less sense than a thief,
It defies even political science.

WHO ARE YOU ROOTING FOR?[52]

If we understand what it should mean,
Many dangers in this story are seen.
In a route, or no root?
Your risk is acute!
But there's also danger in routine!

50. Mark 3:17.
51. Mark 3:22–27.
52. Mark 4:1–9.

FIGURE OUT THE FIGURE[53]

To understand the parable's art,
Each hearer must work for his part.
No harvest is found
In unplowed, fallow ground.
Mere furrowed brows, or furrow the heart?

A BRIGHT IDEA[54]

Like plants that must wait all the night
To photosynthesize when it's light,
No good fruit is made
If we're in the shade.
God's enlightening must be our delight.

PARDON ME, HAVE YOU GOT THE KINGDOM OF GOD?[55]

If you relish His teaching, it's evident:
Mustard your strength, go see where He went,
Pursue with vim
And ketchup with Him,
To learn what the parables condi-ment.

53. Mark 4:10–12.
54. Mark 4:21–25.
55. Mark 4:30–32.

WHY HE CROSSED THE LAKE[56]

With fatigue Jesus became stricken.
"Let us cross the lake and thus quicken
Our way to the far side."
That's why the ride;
Also, to make the apostles less chicken.

CURING[57]

"When locked up I broke out—bam!
Possessed by a legion I am!"
When Jesus cast them out,
All knew beyond doubt,
He healed the man, and deviled the ham.[58]

HAM ON RYE?[59]

Mark will oft start one story, then switch.
It keeps interest at a high pitch.
By showing a link,
It should make us think.
Man—crowd—man forms an "I scream" sandwich.[60]

---

56. Mark 4:35–41.

57. Mark 5:1–17.

58. The miracle of turning the swine to water. The demons' request to be sent into the swine was a pig picking. Events showed that the demonic intent was hogwash. Perhaps they thought that possession was nine-tenths of the law, though possession might explain more than nine tenths of celebrity lawyers.

59. Mark 5:2–20.

60. The literary technique is referred to as a Markan sandwich.

COUNTING ON GOD[61]

If as messengers, you are His picks,
The Lord won't leave you in a fix.
As you go two by two
One tu-nic each will do.
But packing two tunics He does nix.

OUTHERODING HEROD[62]

"Herod," "Herodias:"[63] you must check
Who's who, for their family was a wreck,
Their rival schemes
A TV soap writer's dreams,
And they inbred worse than a redneck.

WOE, JOHNNY![64]

Hear—but not heed—Herod[65] would,
But his wife/niece would kill John if she could.
When by vow he was stuck,
John's life he did chuck.
Yet burial showed Johnny B.'s good.

---

61. Mark 6:7–9.

62. Mark 6:17.

63. And several other names repeated in the family.

64. Mark 6:21–29.

65. Herod Antipas, a son of Herod the Great, half-brother of Herod-Philip (Herodias's first husband) as well as half-brother of Herodias' father. Her brother was Herod Agrippa I.

TRUE GYROS[66]

After feeding the crowd, each disciple
Gathered leftovers, each basket full.
Ere long they might wish
No more flat bread and fish,
But we learn: human strength is just pitaful.

GETTING TO THE HEART OF THE MATTER[67]

"I keep all these rules," we self-flatter.
But such boasts are mere idle chatter.
In truth, we are fickle,
Which puts us in a pickle.
I'm not kosher: my heart's what's the matter.

HANDY ADVICE[68]

Don't be trapped and in your sin drown,
But keep focused to win the true crown.
If a piece of you
Turns from what is true,
Saving souls should win out, hands down.

66. Mark 6:43.
67. Mark 7:19–20.
68. Mark 9:43.

TOE THE LINE[69]

What is life's most important goal?
It's not being externally whole.
Better to be defeeted
Than to be defeated;
Your soul is worth more than your sole.

WHAT KEPT YOU?[70]

Though placed too high in some modern views,
Kids were nobodies to the ancient Jews.
Thus the invitation
The disciples did stun.
But we next see that the proud will refuse.

MEASURED ENTHUSIASM[71]

"Teacher, how can I go up?
Commandments, I've kept since a pup."
Possessions possessed him,
And divesting distressed him:
The ruler did not measure up.

---

69. Mark 9:45.
70. Mark 10:14–17.
71. Mark 10:17–31.

SHORT-TERM INVESTMENT[72]

When the young ruler was put to the test,
He thought present riches were best.
His way to calculate
Determined his fate:
One hundred fold? Not enough interest.

HOT SEATS?[73]

"Teacher, best seats we would gain."
"That, you cannot, but will share my pain."
To drink cup of wrath,
Sharing death is the path.
"We're able!" But soon failed under the strain.

TURNING TO AN OLD LEAF[74]

Springtime promised sweet buds to spare,
But underneath, branches were bare.
Each promising leaf
Proved fruitless. In brief,
They could not hide that nothing was there.

72. Mark 10:21–31.
73. Mark 10:35–40.
74. Mark 11:12–14; Gen 3:7.

LEARNING THE WRONG LESSON[75]

"From God? That just could not be!
But we were caught by a dichotomy . . . "
"Your motive's not true,
Your 'di'chotomy, too.
You certainly have not caught a Me."

COINING A PHRASE[76]

A trick question about their taxation
Was designed to offend the whole nation.
But checking the image
Resolved the scrimmage:
It was not taxing without representation.

RAISING A DEAD QUESTION[77]

They thought their argument was amazin':
"No way you could make sense of raisin'!
See, we are so wise!
Won't his pulse rise?"
But instead, Christ rose to the occasion.

75. Mark 11:31; 12:13–17.
76. Mark 12:13–17.
77. Mark 12:18–27.

A FIRM AFFIRMATION[78]

In his human strength, Peter tried
To remain close to his Lord's side.
Resolve did not avail,
For he soon did fail,
But Jesus the denial soon denied.

IN CIDER TRADING[79]

"Seize the fruit and you'll rule your own palace!"
Was a lie, told from evil and malice.
When we take what we please,
Bitter juices we squeeze,
But it was Christ who would drain the chalice.

WHO IS HE FOR?[80]

"Save yourself!"—yet He must not break
From the cross if our sin He would take.
To take us in
And make us kin,
He must be forsaken for our sake.

78. Mark 14:26–31.
79. Mark 14:36.
80. Mark 15:29–32.

ROCK IN ROLE[81]

His followers hid in fear and doubt:
This could not be the triumphal route!
In their silence,
Who gives evidence?
Tomb and door: it's the stones that cry out.[82]

SILENT TREATMENT[83]

Zechariah for a son was pining,
But was so much to his lack resigning
As to doubt a sign.
So, to put him in line,
He spent the next nine months signing.

MANGER DANGER[84]

In a barn's[85] no distinguished position,
Despite much sentimental tradition.
From heaven to earth,
A plain, humble birth,
Put our Lord in a stable condition.

81. Mark 16:1–8.

82. Luke 19:40.

83. Luke 1.

84. Luke 2:7.

85. The text only says "manger," which could be in an ordinary house as well as a stable, but smell and noise would be similar.

GOODWILL TO MEN[86]

By God's love our greed is arrested.
"Got two suits? Then give one!" we are tested.
If you give it away
You then can say
"Both then and now, I am di-vested."

A LEAP OF BAD FAITH[87]

Satan tries to spread confusion
By taking verses and misusin'.
God's protection
Isn't for foolish fun:
Such a claim is jumping to contusion.

MARKET PRICE[88]

"Well, I'll cast out the nets if you wish,
Though we won't catch enough for one dish."
"Now, you'll begin
To be fishers of men!"
To go back to their old jobs would be sell fish.

86. Luke 3:11.
87. Luke 4:9–12.
88. Luke 5:4–11.

A CROSS WORD PUZZLE[89]

The disciples were oft at a loss,
For they retained much of their dross.
They couldn't use
The most basic clues:
One came down, and won a cross.

AS READ BY FRED[90]

Claims to care will quickly fall flat
If they prove to just be idle chat.
Would you be a neighbor?
At faithfulness labor;
To God's word you must say, "Roger that!"

OVERSTUFFED[91]

The rich fool, he died in his sin.
No construction could he begin.
He had loads of stuff
And thought it enough,
But he was not barn again.

89. Luke 9:23, 44–45.
90. Luke 10:29–37.
91. Luke 12:16–21.

STEWARD'S FOLLY[92]

"My master will be gone quite a while,
So I will start living in style!"
How did he begin
His lapse into sin?
It started with living in denial.

BEST GUEST[93]

Jesus blesses each one who sees
That our hope is in falling to knees,
Pleading for grace which
Was spurned by the "rich."
Only beggars can be choosees.

DO YOU CAROB-OUT ME?[94]

Days of plenty and parties long past,
Compared fodder and father at last.
Thought turned to deed,
He threw aside the feed,
Thus originating the podcast.

---

92. Luke 12:45–46.

93. Luke 14:16–24.

94. Luke 15:13–17. Carob is a plausible, though not definitive, identification of the pods used as pig food in the parable. Leaving the pigs behind was un-sty-lish.

OFF BASE[95]

Called the parable of the prodigal son,
Though the elder must also be won,
The tale is a hit,
For we see in it
That the younger can make a home run.

COOK BOOKS[96]

At accounting, he was quite slick,
But his master caught on to the trick.
By giving discounts
On all the accounts,
Of friends he soon had his pick.

AS NOT SEEN ON TV[97]

"My riches clearly demonstrate how
Much God keeps on blessing me. Wow!"
Thus he did name
Health and wealth, and claim:
Dives[98] experienced his best life now.

95. Luke 15:11–32.

96. Luke 16:1–13.

97. Luke 16:19–25.

98. Traditional name for the rich man contrasted with Lazarus. Dives ended up in a low dive.

READ THE SIGN[99]

You must learn from what you have read,
Not demand miracles for more "cred."
Don't stand and sigh
Looking into the sky:
You should go look it up instead!

TAXING BELIEF[100]

A Pharisee said, "I'm a giant
At goodness!" in a boring rant
That was unphair, I see
To a publican. He
Judged aright with a public "can't."[101]

BIBLICAL DWARVES[102]

Zacchaeus was short, that is right.
Can you think of others? You might
Mention "Knee-high-miah"
But even he's higher
Than Bildad, who was a "Shoe-height."[103]

99. Luke 16:29–31; Acts 1:11.

100. Luke 18:8–14.

101. Whereas the Pharisee's prayer was public cant.

102. Luke 19:3; Neh 1:1; Job 2:11. Cf. one of Pa Grape's cues in Nawrocki, *Autotainment*.

103. And Peter, James, and John were small enough to sleep on their watch.

SOCIAL CLIMBER[104]

Zack's earthly wealth proved a bore,
He sought for treasures that endure.
Not being big,
He climbed a fig,
Because he had grown sick of "more!"[105]

TALENT SHOW[106]

The third servant just didn't get
His task: to invest, not a pit.[107]
He should have obeyed
Like Pharoah's daughter's maid—
At the bank, she drew out a small prophet.

ALL MITE-Y[108]

Jesus gave us all new light
On giving. For at first sight,
Someone might call
Her gift a mite small,
But by percents it was dynamite.[109]

---

104. Luke 19:2–8.

105. The sycamore tree of eastern North America is a plane tree (*Platanus*), whereas 1 Kgs 10:27 shows that the sycamore fig of the Bible was a plain tree.

106. Luke 19:11–27; Exod 3:5–6.

107. He thought it was a savings and loam.

108. Luke 21:1–4.

109. She showed her agreement with Jesus' teaching by giving a cent. His approval was a pennydiction.

READING BETWEEN THE LINES[110]

In hindsight the disciples seem dense.[111]
Their Bible gave much evidence:
From sin Christ would save
Through life past the grave,
But they missed the cross reference.

SPIRITUAL INFANTS[112]

Of decisions, there's been a spate,
But Jesus must now educate.
After the first turning,
There remains much learning.
Spiritually, he's just a neo-Nate.

FLAT OR FLATTERY BREAD[113]

He came to bring us to God's love
But we try in our molds Him to shove.
"King of free food!" they said,
"Lawyer!" "Rebel!" "No—bread?!"
Thus showing He was naan[114] of the Above.

110. Luke 24:25.

111. This is unfair, as we are benefitting from the explanations that their puzzlement elicited.

112. John 1:45–51.

113. John 6.

114. Flat bread familiar to frequenters of Indian restaurants.

SELECTIVE MEMORY[115]

"A prophet! Like Moses—to deliver!"
But Moe had many jobs in his quiver.
They were not set free
To indulge their fancy:
Moses was also judge and lawgiver.

ILL-BREAD[116]

Seeing Jesus, the eager crowd rushes,
But to heed His teaching none hushes.
Such a handout?
He must have clout!
Bread of life? They chose bread and circuses.

A DRY COMMENT[117]

"God's kingdom is within," He'd explain,
But this would not reach a closed brain.
"Crown him!" they sing,
But He's already King!
He showed His reign by reining the rain.

---

115. John 6:14.
116. John 6:14–15.
117. John 6:15–21.

YUM—KIPPER![118]

They should have been with insight imbued,
But identifying true needs remained crude.
Would covering sin
Or covered dish win?
Atonement ranked behind getting food.

YOU CAN TAKE IT, BUT CAN YOU DISH IT OUT?[119]

How can we become Jesus's brothers?
One part this passage discovers:
If on Him we feed,
It fulfills our need.
By serving Himself, Christ serves others.

WATERS OF TESTING[120]

When words need hard thought to make sense,
The responses give the evidence.
It cuts like a knife:
The water of life—
Do you drink deeply or merely rinse[121]?

118. John 6:26. Kippers are salt-preserved fish familiar to consumers of Wodehousian English breakfasts. Yom Kippur is the Day of Atonement, the word for atonement deriving from a root meaning to cover.

119. John 6:52–54.

120. John 6:59–69. Cf. Massah (Exod 17:7).

121. Gargle wouldn't rhyme.

SHEEPISH[122]

Christ's shepherding we often spurn.
How long it takes us to learn
Not to be a proud ram,
Running off on the lam,
But to humbly make a ewe turn![123]

MAKE ME A CHANNEL NO. 5[124]

It was a deed of great self-denial:
Lids that reclose were future, quite a while.
Once broken, use it all.
Thus, there was no call
For rebuke—one cannot re-vial.

PLANTED[125]

Of ourselves, we're shriveled and needy;
Any growth would be fruitlessly weedy.
It seems quite a pain
Going against our grain,
But He must break down all that's seedy.

---

122. John 10:1–16.
123. If we're stiff-necked and won't bend, we can't be in the sheep fold.
124. John 12:1–8.
125. John 12:24–25.

UNSOILED[126]

Peter thought the washing to spurn. He
Of his need still had to learn. The
Daily dust must go
Or else he'd show
The traces of a sedimental journey.[127]

HOLY GROUND[128]

Our own strength leads us to defeats—
We will slip and beat our retreats.
Through the Lord is found
Grip on firmer ground
As if with a good pair of cleats.

THIS BUD'S YOU[129]

"Be a branch if you want to be Mine,
For love and tendril care's My design."
You do not know Him,
If cut off from phloem.
We must trust Him, for He is de Vine.

126. John 13:5–10.

127. At first Peter, though dry, had wet feet; his next idea was all wet. The need only to wash the feet was foreshadowed by Jeroboams I's father—he was the son of Nebath.

128. John 14:26.

129. John 15:1–2.

ROCKY II[130]

Persecution brought many a groan,
Yet the church knew that they weren't alone.
The LORD had been through
Both this and more, too:
Without sin, He forecast the first stone.

HOLD OFF HOLDING ON[131]

On the third day, from death our Lord rose.
From this, new relationship flows.
"I'm not static—don't cling!
Great change I now bring.
Time to grasp at My teaching, not toes."

FAITH AND HOP[132]

The healed man's joyous effusion
Was putting the crowd in confusion.
As the man leaped about
With many a shout,
Peter helped them to jump to conclusions.

130. John 15:18—16:4.
131. John 20:17.
132. Acts 3.

WHAT WOULD JESUS DRIVE?[133]

You'd choose a good vehicle. So,
The apostles, as you probably know
Were all in one Accord,
But what about the Lord?
From the Spanish—"*Toma mi Yugo*."[134]

SWEET BUY AND BUY[135]

"God's soldier" can be a very
Apt metaphor for a missionary.
But the love of the Lord
Is the chief reward.
Don't seek to be a mercenary.

A CLEAR PATH[136]

His pursuit would stand no delay;
Believers he'd arrest and slay.
He'd purge this error
By spreading terror:
To Saul, Christians were in the Way.

---

133. Acts 4:24; Matt 11:29–30.

134. "Take my yoke" (or "Take my Yugo"). The Yugo won *Car Talk*'s Worst Car competition, so removal requests are plausible.

135. Acts 8:18–23.

136. Acts 9:1–2.

AT THE END OF HIS ROPE[137]

Once the truth Paul was able to see,
He had to leave town quite quickly.
His friends in the place,
Judged him a basket case,
And hampered him to make him free.[138]

HIDES AND SEEK[139]

In Joppa, Peter needed some space,
So the Lord led him to a good base.
It was in this manner:
He stayed with a tanner,
Thus giving him a hiding place.

KNOCK, AND THE DOOR WILL OPEN
. . . EVENTUALLY[140]

Herod was not going to win.
Though he'd locked Peter up in the pen.
God set Peter free,
Surprising many.
But once out, Peter couldn't get in![141]

---

137. Acts 9:23–25.

138. The strategy for smuggling him out was over the top.

139. Acts 9:43.

140. Acts 12:3–16.

141. Perhaps the first knock-knock-knock-knock joke. On finding him gone, no doubt the guards were in a Peter panic. After this incident, Herod Agrippa I's persecution petered out.

THE DIET OF WORMS[142]

Agrippa seemed to fare quite well,
But these verses show how he fell.
In judgment, his striker
Was like a big biker,
For he was a helminth's[143] angel.

MERCURIAL[144] TEMPERAMENT[145]

"Your pagan enthusiasm please curb! We
Are men!" This turn did disturb the
Lystrian crowd.
Things soon got loud,
But demolition won't keep Paul from Derbe.[146]

REWRITTEN[147]

Though Mark's cousin Barnabas had pull,
Paul of doubts about Mark became full.[148]
But in years to come,
Useful he'd become.
The turnaround was re-Markable.

---

142. Acts 12:20–23.

143. Helminth—a worm, especially a parasitic one. Perhaps Agrippa's heart was strangely wormed.

144. The Lystrians' Hermes-neutics were in error.

145. Acts 14:11–20.

146. Asian Derbe, not Kentucky.

147. Acts 15:37–39; 2 Tim. 4:11.

148. Paul regarded his departure from the first missionary journey as a mark against him. This is a rare case of P, B, and J not sticking together.

EPIC FAIL[149]

Versus troubles under the sun,
They pursued happiness and fun.
In vain the Epicure
Sought a happy cure:
At the end of he-donism, he's done.

WHAT BUGS YOU?[150]

To newsfeed addicts, it's no shock:
Athenians to novelties flock.
Running like a rabbit
To news was their habit,
Always demanding, "What's up, doc?"

POETIC JUSTICE[151]

Paul had extensive learning stowed,
Which proved useful on down the road.
Cultural learning
To the table bring:
A hearing earned on a Grecian ode.[152]

149. Acts 17:18.
150. Acts 17:21.
151. Acts 17:28.
152. Keats, "Grecian", 194–5.

ANY STORM IN A PORT[153]

O'er the isthmus ships were hauled sea to sea.
Meanwhile, their crews were all free.
Restraint doesn't cleave
To tars on shore leave:
Roman sailors were all quite *nautae*.[154]

HAIR RAISING[155]

We don't know precisely what spurred
Paul's promise. But we know from the Word
Something of how
He fulfilled his vow:
By deferring being defurred.

A GHASTLY MISTAKE[156]

Their talk had a familiar ring,
But something seemed to be missing.
When pressed for detail,
Their knowledge did fail—
Their grasp of theology was a-Pauline.

153. Acts 18:1–10.

154. Efforts to cut a canal through the isthmus at Corinth (thus saving ships from having to circle southern Greece) had been unsuccessful, so instead cargo and even small ships were slowly hauled over a track across the land. This saved total travel time and gave the crew a few days' vacation. This rhyme requires the nineteenth-century British pronunciation, not our best modern understanding of actual spoken Latin. The reassurance of Acts 18:10 was relevant in light of Corinth's reputation—it's been suggested that Paul's catalogs of sin in Romans could have been inspired by looking out the window while in Corinth. In reality, such lists are also a common part of both Jewish and Roman criticism of popular pagan immorality of the day, with no need of a specific inspiration.

155. Acts 18:18.

156. Acts 19:1–7.

SONS OF SCEVA OR OF GOD?[157]

They claimed the power of the Jewish nation,
But fared poorly in the altercation.
No faith, just a name,
Gave not power but shame,
As was shown in the demon-stration.

UH-OH, SILVER AWAY![158]

To a call for action the crowds stream,
But achieving a goal's but a dream.
In the great uproar,
Few know what it's for,
And just yell that Diana is supreme.[159]

NIGHT WATCH[160]

Freely God gives, but Tyche would take.
Eutychus[161] learned this from his mistake.
He got in a lurch
By sleeping in church,
Leading him to a Lucky break.

---

157. Acts 19:13–16.

158. Acts 19:24–41. Demetrius was afraid that business would drop off so much that he'd need a Loan Arranger. If the populace were no longer fooled by idolatry, he'd be an unmasked man.

159. Diana in the KJV is the Roman equivalent of Artemis of the Greeks. In turn, application of the Greek name "Artemis" to the Ephesian deity actually celebrated there was also looking for rough equivalence. Despite the discrepancy between the Greek virgin huntress and the fertility goddess of Asia, such syncretism was common and posed a challenge for the exclusive claims of the gospel. For example, Gnosticism sought to merge bits of Judaism and Christianity with aspects of Greek thought. Demetrius would be pleased to know that Diana and the Supremes have some silver recordings in the UK, but might not like that the fact that silver ranks below gold and platinum in that system.

160. Acts 20:7–12.

161. From eu- (true) and Tyche, goddess of luck. Thus his fall was Mr. Fortune's misfortune.

CONVEYOR BELT[162]

The future was given a map in
Paul, whom rulers would clap in
Jail—for thus
Spoke Agabus,
Showing what was bound to happen.

IN ORDER[163]

A peace offering Paul did bring;
His call he would not be dodging.
In the faithful we see
True fraternity,
For Paul had a Mnasonic lodging.

PRE-HEARSE-AL[164]

They would kill Paul for imagined terrors.
Suspicion, not truth, their claim mirrors.
"Away now with him!"
The crowd yelled with vim.
Though he lived, the Romans were Paul bearers.

162. Acts 21:4–14.
163. Acts 21:15–17.
164. Acts 21:27–36.

INSIDE KNOWLEDGE[165]

To Pharisaism, he was no alien;
The strictest sort, Gamalielian.
He advanced in his studies
Beyond his buddies,
'Til his words were sesquipedalian.[166]

MALTA MILK?[167]

"An escaped con seems to get a break,
But soon Justice her vengeance will take!"
Yet a bite from an adder
To Paul did not matter;
It seemed just a vanilla snake.

DEFORMING BY CONFORMING[168]

No one can claim to be wholly true.
If we're judged by our works,[169] we are through.
Worldly ways show
The wrong way to go:
In Rome, do not do as Romans do.

165. Acts 22:3; Gal 1:14.

166. A similar limerick was not quite successfully assembled by a character in Dorothy L. Sayers' *Murder Must Advertise*.

167. Acts 28:3–5.

168. Rom 1–3. Being deformed and conformed to the world, we need to be informed and reformed by the Spirit to enter an ongoing life of being transformed into Christ's likeness and performing the works that God calls us to, thereby changing from our former ways to the purpose for which we were formed. Thus, we can consider Romans to be a form letter.

169. In Latin, "man works" is homo facit. Aptly, in classical pronunciation, that would be "fake-it".

WORKS OUT[170]

From the time of Adam and of Seth,
Men labor until their last breath
To earn righteousness,
But our fallen mess
Makes such effort just working to death.

UNEARNED INTEREST[171]

For salvation we do naught of our own.
God alone changes our hearts of stone.
Towards Him we are driven;
Even belief is given:
We are saved just by faith—a loan.[172]

ADAM UP[173]

Though we were all self-centered jerks,
We can now enjoy gracious perks:
The covenant of grace
Puts Christ in our place.
By His fulfillment, the covenant works.

170. Rom 2–7.

171. Rom 3:24.

172. Not, of course, in the sense that we could pay it back, but that it is entirely borrowed (cf. "Can I borrow a tissue to blow my nose?"). Instead of the Loan Office, perhaps one should think of Accounts Prayable.

173. Rom 5:12–21.

GONE TO POT[174]

If God chooses some who have spurned
His love, so that they are turned
Back to what's best,
What of the rest?
As vessels, their judgment's not unurned.

THE RIGHT OUTLOOK[175]

We're called in, but then God does send.
Outreach is part of the church's end,
Not a closed "in" box
With many firm locks:
The message does no good when unopened.

PLOTTING IN VAIN[176]

"Lots of rites will force God to pay us
Attention." "Follow law, that way, thus
God owes us a favor."
Of self these schemes savor—
They made a *machina ex Deus*.[177]

---

174. Rom 9:22.

175. Rom 10:14–15.

176. Rom 10:30–33.

177. *Deus ex machina*, "God from a machine," is a literary plot failing where the contrived situation is such a mess that the resolution is basically an abrupt and implausible miracle. Although the mess humanity is in does require miraculous intervention, this solution was integrated into the plan from before the beginning.

DOUGH RE: ME[178]

From the first, our leavening has proceeded,
But there's no grounds for becoming conceited.
Even the least
Rise comes from yeast.
To fill our roll, God's work is kneaded.

RESTRUCTURED[179]

To turn us, from our ways, towards heaven,
And cleanse us from Adamic leaven,
We must confess
Our bankrupt mess
To move on from chapter eleven.

THE KINDEST CUT OF ALL[180]

At "living sacrifice" we should falter:
That's not a mere yoke nor a halter.
God claims our all,
Despite many a fall,
As we keep crawling back off the altar.

178. Rom 11:16a.
179. Rom 1–11.
180. Rom 12:1.

ALL ROADS LEAD THERE[181]

Paul's trip to Rome had not yet begun
When a skid made his plans come undone.
Though there was no snow,
With chains he did go:
The road to Rome was a rocky one.

STRANGERS AND ALIENS[182]

Many hope a miracle to find,
Thinking it would prove faith in their mind.[183]
Yet those on site
Oft ignored the light.
Take close encounters of the Word kind.

ARSON LUPIN[184]

With a solid foundation we're blessed.
"Construct with God's promise" is best,
With gems of the law,
Not with our own straw.
No huff and puff: flame is the test.

181. Rom 15:22–32; Acts 21:27—28:31.

182. 1 Cor 1:22–24.

183. Instead of letting their yes be yes and no be no, they demanded omen and amen.

184. 1 Cor 3:10–15. Arsène Lupin is the antihero of a French series of stories about a gentleman burglar, cf. *loup*, a wolf, traditionally associated with testing of edifices made of straw.

TROUBLE BREWING[185]

By pride, we are easily fleeced.
Do not act like some senseless beast!
Cast out all sin!
Don't let growth begin!
Such deeds are the mark of the yeast.

APHRODITE CALLIPYGOS[186]

In Corinth, the prospects were bright
If you wanted to party all night.
Venus and Bacchus
Helped make it raucous—
No wisdom from that hindsight.

OVERHAND SERVE[187]

"We're big shots and all better than you!"
Paul serves rightly, better pedigree, too.
So self-commendation
Just brings condemnation,
But God greatly benefits you.

185. 1 Cor 5:2–8.

186. 1 Cor 6:9–11. Callipygos was a particular designation of Aphrodite as worshipped in Corinth, and is what wearers of thong swimsuits apparently fancy themselves to be. Actually, thongs give the appearance of magnipygosity, not callipygosity. Given her vanity, Aphrodite Callipygos was probably fond of her rear-view mirror. As Proverbs 31:30 points out, such charm is de seat full.

187. 2 Cor 10; 11:16–33.

WHO CAN STAND IT?[188]

Theological learning's value is grand;
You may think you've got it all in hand.
But if knowledge swells pride,
This fact you can't hide:
It's proof that you don't under-stand.

BRIDGING DIVIDES[189]

To build up the Body, God chose
Variety of gifts to dispose.
All olfactory:
What good would that be?
Such a thing, no body nose.[190]

GONG SHOW[191]

Word and deeds, though giving no regrets,
Do no good, if love one forgets.
Thus Paul does warn:
Don't toot your own horn.
Kind hearts are more than cornets.[192]

---

188. 1 Cor 10:12.

189. 1 Cor 12:12–21.

190. Our functioning in the body requires the Spirit's work, so there is a place for *extra nos*. (Luther used that Latin phrase emphasizing the role of grace.)

191. 1 Cor 13:1.

192. Tennyson, "Lady Clara Vere de Vere", 158.

DON'T TAKE IT FOR A SPIN[193]

Plain truth should be all our diction;
Careful study to build conviction.
Glitzy PR[194]
From God's will is far:
Steer clear of all pulpit fiction.

SWADDLING[195]

The Corinthian flock had young sheep.
So they needed a nursery to keep.
The lesson learned then,
Proved again and again,
"We shall all be changed; but not all sleep."

ACHILLES' HEAL?[196]

Our own works keep making things worse!
Could anything reverse death's dark curse?
But One Who is life
Came into the strife!
He passed death's gates as a Trojan hearse.

---

193. 1 Cor 15:15; 1 Tim 1:7.

194. Public Relations, stereotypically resorted to when the public is too aware of the truth.

195. 1 Cor 15:51.

196. 1 Cor 15:54–57.

TO NO A-VEIL[197]

A fading glow from when Moses met
With God was sort of a veiled threat,
A warning that we
Face the holy;
But now for unveiled access we're set.

UNCONFORMITY[198]

Metamorphosis, but moth or bee
Is less close than in geology:
It takes heat, pressure,
And time to address your
Need to be transformed[199] to be holy.

INTO THE WARDROBE[200]

Through trials and testing, God will hone
Us 'til we can call clean robes our own.
For our new dress,
Truly permanent press,
Won't fit 'til we're fully groan.

197. 2 Cor 3:13–16.

198. 2 Cor 3:18; Rom 12:2.

199. In both verses, the Greek for "transformed" is metamorphoō. Metamorphic rocks often are found under a geological unconformity, where their surface has been reshaped by things above such as weather. Metasomatism is an even better metaphor, as it is when the rock is transformed not just by heat and pressure, but also from chemicals coming from outside the rock.

200. 2 Cor 5:1–5.

TEMP AGENCY[201]

Look around; there is much evidence
That "is" and "ought" have much divergence.
When that is known,
There's many a groan,
For the troubles that we see are in-tents.

TALK—SHOW?[202]

Of credentials they had fine lists;
Their rhetoric was not to be missed;
But a proud, loveless life
Bred quarrels and strife:
No good fruit; merely tell-evangelists.

ARE YOU SURE?[203]

In faith, Paul's assurance would not fall,
But his insurance bill might be tall:
Shipwreck, arrest,
By beating distressed—
Such as these were the perils of Paul.[204]

---

201. 2 Cor 5:1–5.

202. 2 Cor 10–12.

203. 2 Cor 11:21–33.

204. Somehow, such activities are not on the itineraries of advertised "Life of Paul" tourist trips. Paul certainly would not have wasted money on an insurance policy that did not cover acts of God.

A THORNY PROBLEM[205]

Paul's weakness did self-disappoint,
'Til with meaning God did it anoint.
Weakness, at length,
Shows forth God's strength.
After three times, Paul then got the point.

ADDRESS UNKNOWN[206]

Destination north or south,[207] there's a chance.
On content, not hearers, take your stance.
But why was a Gaul
In Asia at all?
They sought Anatolia France.

A STAR FIGHTER[208]

To legalism, he could never agree. A
Pharisaic past helped Paul to see a
Real threat—no fiction,
Nor merely friction:
Paul had his battle scars, Galatia.[209]

---

205. 2 Cor 12:7–10.

206. Gal 1:2.

207. The province of Galatia was named for the Gauls who lived in the northern part of the province, far from most other Celtic populations, but in New Testament times the province also included southern areas of other ethnicities. Acts records Paul visiting southern Galatia. There is no definite evidence of his visiting the more remote and less populous north, though some older commentators favored a northern destination for the letter. As Anatole France (noted French essayist and author) joined the Communist party late in life, he probably didn't care who Galatians was addressed to.

208. Gal 1:11—2:21.

209. Some peculiarities in the plot of "Battlestar Galactica" reflect its inspiration from Mormonism.

WORK IT OUT[210]

One could get confused by what both said,
If context is not carefully read.
From Paul we see,
Faithless works are deadly;
From James, faith that works not is dead.

PELAGIC PELAGIAN[211]

Saved by grace is the core of our creed,
But is there no role for our deed?
Don't we do our part?
Yes, that's salvation's heart:
It's our works that create the need.

PRINTS OF PEACE[212]

A secretary might do the addressing,
But Paul took the pen for expressing,
With his large script,
How he wished them equipped,
Writing in the font[213] of every blessing.

---

210. Gal 2:16; Jas 2:17.
211. Gal 3.
212. Gal 6:11.
213. Maybe Times New Romans.

CHANGING ROLLS[214]

Of our sins we grow ever fonder;
Each into his own way does wander.
We deserve no pardon—
Our hearts we did harden,
Yet we're there when parole's called up yonder.

CALLOUT[215]

From the world, we now form a new nation.
Things that we, too, once chased, we may shun.
God's way we can heed
In thought, word, and deed.
We're called together, but no more con vocation.

NOT FOR THUMPING[216]

Not theatrics, dramatically gasped,
But God's word, in our hand is clasped.
It's no club, but a sword;
Not ours—of the Lord.
It cuts us if not properly grasped.

214. Eph 2:1–10.
215. Eph 4:20–32.
216. Eph 6:17.

CHAINED LETTER[217]

Rome's ways clashed with Christianity,
In spirit, not militarily.
No calls for revolt,
But to mentally *volte*
Face: with some caution, Paul spoke guardedly.

LEARN WHAT'S INSIDE[218]

Woe or weal, Paul did not wince.
Trouble to his armor made no dents.
Thus, he gives a list
To tell us the gist
Of his secret—a table of contents.

ANGELS WE HAVE MADE TOO HIGH[219]

Before angels one might well quake,[220]
But they're servants, sent for our sake.
If they are adored,
Instead of the Lord,
You've made a colossal mistake.

---

217. Phil 1:13.
218. Phil 4:11–13.
219. Col 1:8–18.

220. Many modern images of angels don't match with the fact that they usually had to start their conversations with humans with "Fear not!" (Lewis, *Screwtape*, ix). However, that doesn't justify shaky theology.

FINDING THE FASTEST ROOT[221]

Though for progress we need the Word's light,
Mixing metaphors sounds quite a sight.
We're called to be
Like a mobile tree:
Being rooted so as to walk aright.

LAW OUT OF ORDER[222]

They thought they were getting ahead
By conforming to ways that are dead!
Adding in works
Does not earn perks,
But instead cuts us off from the Head.

WELL-ROUNDED THEOLOGY?[223]

"Paul says here that I am a winner
If I eat the most at a church dinner!"
No, you must heed
Warnings about greed;
Ascetic or glutton, I'm a sinner.

---

221. Col 2:6–7.
222. Col 2:16–19.
223. Col 2:16–23.

DYING TO KNOW[224]

An answer they all sought to find:
Will those who sleep be in a bind?
No; believers all
Will hear the great call.
Those not quick won't be left behind.[225]

MIND YOUR OWN BUSINESS[226]

In our callings, to honor God, we
Work well—that's nothing odd. He
Seeks busy living
In serving and giving,
Not in being a busybody.

URGENT BROADCAST[227]

In sound doctrine we must always rest,
Not adding anything to sound "best."
Our witness is bad
If to God we add;
This is attest, this is only attest.

---

224. 1 Thess 4:13–18.

225. Although it's often claimed that delay of the parousia was a major problem for the early church, passages on the topic generally emphasize that the time is not known. Similarly, concern about people dying before Jesus's return is no proof of late date—the question would occur to any group that included elderly, infirm, or mortal members.

226. 2 Thess 3:10–11.

227. 1 Tim 1:3–7.

TRUE AND FALSE PROFITS[228]

Paul admitted that godliness brings gain,
But immediately he had to explain.
Being content
Is what Paul meant.
Those who chase mammon only gain pain.

TRAINING TRACKS[229]

Scripture is indeed perspicacious,
But the task of study still does face us.
We often get caught
Trusting our own thought.
What errors we make! Goodness gracious!

SOUND COUNSEL OR ECHO CHAMBER?[230]

In questing for wisdom, do not rest.
"Do I like it?" is not a sound test.
A pandering voice
Is a popular choice,
But you seek out those who know best.

228. 1 Tim 6:5–10.
229. 2 Tim 3:14–16.
230. 2 Tim 4:3–5.

DON'T FORGET TO WRITE![231]

Cloak and dagger tales may readers win;
Paul knew that sword has less might than pen.
Yet this mighty word
Was the sword of the Lord,
Mightier than the pen Paul was in.

101 STATIONS?[232]

In each place, Titus served and taught. He
Persevered through each controversy.
What he did in Crete,
We can repeat,
But on Dalmatia, our info's quite spotty.

TRULY FALSE[233]

Cretans all are liars, we know,
For one of their own told us so.
But if he lies, too,
Then their word is true . . .
Thus round and round we can go.

---

231. 2 Tim 4:13.
232. 2 Tim 4:10; Titus 1:5.
233. Titus 1:12–13.

WHAT'S THE USE?[234]

Philemon in his slave couldn't see
Any prospect of utility.
He ran off, met Paul;
That changed it all:
Both Onesimus[235] and slavery.

A TRAITOROUS TRADE[236]

Once tasted, if faith you then toss,
Seeming gains prove but greater loss.
There is but one Way;
In this you must stay,
Or commit a heinous double cross.

COMEBACK WIN[237]

The first team was lost; foes did drub—
At perfect obedience we flub.
But God had a plan
Before it began:
It was time to send in the sub.

234. Phlm 1.
235. Paul himself punned on the name (1:11), which means "useful."
236. Heb 6:4–6.
237. Heb 9.

HEART TRANSPLANT[238]

It's clear that the old one is dross.
For a new heart, the stone one we'll toss.
But that operation
Needs a blood donation,
Which only comes from a red cross.

KEEP IN TOUCH[239]

Of God's word, preaching's the carrier,
And fellowship to error is a barrier.
To your great cost,
The message is lost
'Til you enter the service area.

LONGER SERMON, PLEASE[240]

The past saints can show us the way
To live out our faith every day.
Yet they failed, too,
Just as you and I do.
About Jephthah, what *would* you say?!

---

238. Heb 10:19–22; Ezek 11:19.
239. Heb 10:25.
240. Heb 11:32.

BROTH-ERRS[241]

Through faith, we pay heed to God's law.
Do not be a worldling, like Esau.
He did not think
Beyond food and drink,
He had no faith—just what he saw.

COUNT YOUR TRIALS, NAME THEM ONE BY ONE[242]

Take trials as joy, and treasure them up,
Thus you will mature; do not stay a pup.
Though the trial's not fun,
We'll see when it's done,
Like Joy®, it has cleaned the whole cup.

IMAGE-INARY[243]

Doesn't listening prove my election?
No, there's still a chance for defection.
You've seen the mirror,
But still must beware, for
It helps not without further reflection.[244]

---

241. Heb 12:16–17.
242. Jas 1:2; Heb 12:11; Luke 11:39.
243. Jas 1:22–24.
244. Insights from the text must not become oversights in application.

INTENT STAKES[245]

The mirror of the law God did give.
Our looking must be quite intensive.
Not mere intent;
Are deeds evident?
Mere thoughts are just a pen-sieve.

ACTIONS SPEAK LOUDER THAN WORDS[246]

"Go in peace, be warm, and be full!"
Mere words do not help real people.
If your whole boast
Is, "I click and post!"
That warmth is hot air, not noble.[247]

TONGUES OF FIRE[248]

Few consciences do not get pricked
About words that aren't carefully picked.
If your tongue doesn't say
What it oughtn't, each day,
Then most of your troubles are licked.

---

245. Jas 1:25.
246. Jas 2:14–16.
247. It also fails to be no bull.
248. Jas 3:1–12.

THE HOLE TRUTH[249]

"Be holy as I am holy," yes,
But of ourselves, we're an ugly mess.
We must be lowly,
For God makes us holy,
Patching huge holes in our holiness.

CAMPAIGN PROMISE[250]

If votes by the deceased are applied
To elections, then fraud is decried.
But from this we demur:
Our election's secure,
With the vote of the One who has died.

SKATING ON THIN EISEGESIS[251]

In some verses the meaning is missed,
Read Paul aright to get the gist.
The response is soon
To those out of tune:
"To interpret, do not do the twist."

249. 1 Pet 1:16.
250. 2 Pet 1:10.
251. 2 Pet 3:14–17. A slippery slope fallacy.

APPLIED STUDY[252]

Peter found Paul hard to understand.
Now expositors give us a hand:
They help us to see
What the meaning might be,
But to pride that word is hard to stand.

TRUE LOVE[253]

"God is love," is a popular quote,
But the meaning's from context, not by vote:
Follow Him—that's the way
To grow in love each day.
Not that on our whims, He's sure to dote.

MIND THE SIGNS[254]

John preferred not to write but to talk,
But at a short note he won't balk:
"Obey what is right,
Not against the light—
Be sure to keep in the cross walk."

252. 2 Pet 3:15–16.
253. 1 John 4:7–21.
254. 2 John 1:4–12.

LOOK OUT FOR #1[255]

To be first, Diotrephes tried
Words from other teachers to hide.
It worked, in a way:
He's known to this day—
As a deplorable model of pride.

COVERT AGENTS[256]

Brother of James, bond[257]-servant still
Of Christ, warns of those who fulfill
Prophecies of each lout
Who creeps in and spies out.
He shows us that license will kill.

THE BEST DE-FENCE[258]

To keep the whole law, you are failing,
Unless of precautions you're availing.
You'll be all set
With a parapet.
Yet Michael did the right thing through not railing.[259]

---

255. 3 John 1:9.

256. Jude 1:1–23.

257. Cf. the famous ornithologist, James Bond, whose name was used by Ian Fleming.

258. Jude 1:9 KJV; Deut 22:8.

259. Thus not going off the rails.

SEA SICK[260]

Sunny beaches fill without failing,
But not when a storm is assailing![261]
The old monster Yām[262]
With each wave does slam:
Hebrew thought is not of smooth saline.

FUTURE SCHLOCK[263]

God told John of His plans to remind
Us to heed what in His Word we find.
But by predilections
For undue predictions,
Sound exegesis is soon left behind.

WITH HEAT AND VOICE[264]

Interpreters, each with his own twist:
Pre-? Post-? A-? For their mill, this is grist.
"Idealist!" "Futurist!"
"Historicist!" "Preterist!"
The four hoarse men of the apocalypse.

---

260. Jude 1:13a; Rev 21:1b; Job 7:12.

261. Not counting Weather Channel staff and crazy surfers.

262. "Yām" can just mean ocean or sea, but in the surrounding mythologies the Sea was a force of chaos, challenging the gods. Biblical writers took up that imagery to show God as sovereign even over what others thought was an uncontrollable independent power. (Of course, they reject the polytheism of the myths, just as someone like Calvin or Milton would use classical mythology allusions without believing in the Greco-Roman pantheon.)

263. Rev 1:1–3.

264. Rev 1—22.

POST APOCALYPTIC?[265]

Some slipped into complacent grooves. All
Faced threat of judgment and removal.
Sending did avail
Of the Roman mail,[266]
But not all got the stamp of approval.

GREAT EXPECTORATIONS[267]

Spa-like warmth or cold, like a fridge,
But in between's only fit for a midge.
If we taste like the world,
From the Lord we are hurled.
We must not become a spitting image.

VISION IS IN THE EYE OF THE BEHOLDER[268]

Angels have no physicality,
But are spirits affecting reality.
Appearances symbolize:
Their numerous eyes
Aren't why scalloped potatoes are heavenly.

265. Rev 2–3.
266. The cities of the churches are along a Roman postal route.
267. Rev 3:14–16.
268. Rev 4:1–8.

GOOD HOUSEKEEPING?[269]

The time of His judgment will prove full.
The faithless must face their removal.
His own are protected;
The rest are rejected:
Plagues are the seals of disapproval.

SEALED[270] FATE[271]

Babylon to the masses appeals;
Bread, circus, and pleasure, her spiels.
These seals are destroying,
Not a circus enjoying;
They're more like bull elephant seals.[272]

DENSE AND DECADENCE[273]

On judgments the wise ought to ponder
But most stubbornly still chose to wander.
Surely they oughtter
Learn from bitter water,
But absinthe[274] didn't make their hearts fonder.

269. Rev 6.

270. He who has ears to hear, let him hear. (True seals lack external ears, unlike sea lions and certain other pinnipeds.)

271. Rev 6; 17.

272. Male Southern Elephant Seals are the largest marine mammals other than whales, reaching (record size) 7 meters long and 5000 kg. The males are mutually aggressive during the mating season, typically determining dominance by vocalization volume, followed (if necessary) by physical blows and biting.

273. Rev 8:10–11, 9:20–21.

274. A liquor, flavored with wormwood, stereotypically associated with 19th-century dissipation. Decadence suggests ten times as dense as normal.

A MODEL RULER?[275]

Insanely violent, huge ego—these were
How Nero was known, to be sure.
Yet even he did not get
So bad as to fit
This vision of a *grand mal* Caesar.[276]

MARKIN' PRIORITY[277]

"What's the Mark of the Beast?" many wondered,
But far too often we've blundered:
By numbered IDs,
Zip codes, CCVs,
From glory you will not be sundered.[278]

NOT A MATH PROBLEM[279]

Versus the perfection of heaven,
Free of taint of any worldly leaven,
The fallen, in their fix
Can't pass 666,
Never reaching the ideal of seven.[280]

275. Rev 13.

276. A popular preterist model claims that either Nero himself or rumors that he would somehow return are the clear model for the antichrist, but the fact that no early commentator saw the resemblance to Nero makes it seem rather doubtful. No doubt Nero and myriad other tyrants help to inspire John's picture of the culmination of evil rule, but Revelation seems best interpreted as looking both at the then-current situation and into the future.

277. Rev 13:16–18.

278. Nor will personal computers, area codes, home internet, vaccines, or evil vegetarian meat substitutes designed by satanists or the lizard people to turn people into other species so that they can't be saved. (All of those have been hyped as purportedly being the mark of the beast.) What comes out of the heart, not an external label, marks you.

279. Rev 13:18.

280. In mathematics, six is considered a "perfect" number because its

MAMMON[281]

She thought she was loved and in health,
But her foes didn't even need stealth.
Many missed her cash
As they saw from the ash
That smoking was bad for their wealth.

HEATED DEBATE[282]

Many a claim is a fake of a liar,
But do not as they do, nor aspire
To do likewise to them;
For all who join in,
Such sins earn spots in the lake of fire.

PINING FOR HEAVEN[283]

Although the description is quite brief,
The glimpse supersedes all belief.
The trees that are seen
Are all evergreen,
Promising no ending to all our releaf.

---

factors (other than itself) add up to itself: $1+2+3=6$, a rather rare phenomenon (there are only 4 examples under 30 million). However, in traditional Near Eastern symbolism, seven was considered the number symbolizing perfection; some remnant of that belief continues in the popular association of seven with good luck. Thus, six falls short of perfection, and 666 is threefold failure to measure up. As three symbolizes completion, the beast, for all his seeming achievement, is a total failure, contrasting with the myriad sevens of heaven throughout Revelation. Note also that the number of limericks herein exceeds 666.

281. Rev 18.
282. Rev 21:8.
283. Rev 22:2.

APOCRYPHA

THE VOICE OF THE TURTLE[1]

Tobit was a godly old fellow
Who should have relocated his pillow.
His son did well
With Raphael;
Of the other three, the story don a tello.[2]

HEAD START

It was once upon a time,[3] 'tis said,
The Jews were all trembling with dread,
'Til Judith did beguile
Holofernes a while.
Then the townspeople soon got a head.

1. Twain, *Innocents*, 284–5, claimed that one of his fellow travelers was determined to locate a turtle in the Holy Land and hear it sing, based on the King James Version reference to the voice of the turtle (Song 2:12). When he found a turtle it didn't say anything, much to the seeker's annoyance. As the "turtle" in the verse is a turtledove, the reptile's silence is unsurprising.

2. Raphael, Leonardo, Michelangelo, and Donatello are the Teenage Mutant Ninja Turtles.

3. It seems highly unlikely that any Jew would not know that Nebuchadnezzar was king of Babylon, not Assyria, so the opening reference in Judith is probably a deliberate indication of fiction.

MAKING A SPLASH

On Anabaptism, Luther cast aspersion;
But end times fantasy caused diversion:
Second Esdras[4]
Was such a morass
That he deemed that it needed immersion.[5]

HOT TRIO

Nebuchadnezzar, mad at the three,
Sought to make examples, firey.
The heat of the moment
Should put them in foment,
But instead made four-part harmony.[6]

4. Nomenclature of Ezra-related books is complex. "Esdras" is an alternate spelling of Ezra, but in English it is usually applied to the two apocryphal books, 1 Esdras adding the tale of the three guardsmen to a synthesis of parts of 2 Chronicles, Ezra, and Nehemiah, and 2 Esdras purporting to be secret revelation to Ezra. Ezra's bringing a copy of the Law back from Babylon morphed into a legend that the Scriptures had been lost and God dictated to Ezra the full text of all the pre-exilic parts of Scripture. This legend was further enhanced by the claim that God had also given Ezra additional secret revelation, which 2 Esdras claims to provide some of. This ancient legend of Ezra re–producing the text is curiously similar to the modern legend of the Pentateuch, much of Isaiah, *etc.* being exilic or postexilic compositions.

5. However, in baptism by immersion it is customary to also practice emersion, whereas Luther did not retrieve his copy of 2 Esdras out of the Elbe River.

6. The incident of the fiery furnace is, of course, in the canonical text, but the song is apocryphal.

FOSTERING WISDOM[7]

"Comply, or else your song will be
'Woe, Susanna.'" "Don't you lie to me."
The elders' tale
Would surely fail,
For Daniel knew his botany.[8]

NOT FRATERNIZING[9] WITH THE ENEMY

Antiochus Epimanēs[10]
Sought the temple treasury to seize,
And also did seek
To make everyone Greek,
Thus triggering the Maccabees.

7. Way down by the Euphrates River.

8. Daniel was such a popular figure that supplemental legends developed around him. In the tale of Susannah, Daniel pronounces judgment on the dishonest elders by punning on the different type of tree that each put into his version of the lie. Omitting "for" and "his" in the last line would fit the meter of "Oh, Susannah!".

9. Eschewing the Greek system.

10. He claimed the title "Epiphanēs"—"God manifest," obviously blasphemous to the Jews. Epimanēs (madman) was an alternate title used by those outside Antiochus' hearing.

CHURCH HISTORY

CARD-CARRYING HERETICS?

Their cupidity for intellectualness
Led Gnostics into a syncretizing mess.
They're anti-body.
Thereby we see
That Valentinus was truly heartless.[1]

UN-SEEM-LY

"God and man cannot be one, I deem,"
Thus docetists[2] their own ideas esteem.
On Christ, their stance:
"It's mere appearance!"
Thus did their approach split the seam.

---

1. Gnosticism was a mix of ideas promoting the dualistic Greek philosophical tradition of matter=bad, spirit=good. Some mixed this with elements of Christianity, but rejected basic ideas such as the goodness of physical creation, the full humanity of Jesus, and bodily resurrection. This attitude could lead to asceticism (seeking to repress the body) or to license (reasoning that the body is part of the bad stuff being gotten rid of, so whatever actions the body takes do not matter). Both asceticism and license have been problems in the Church at various points, as has being unduly swayed by popular intellectual movements.

2. Docetism, meaning "to seem," claimed that Jesus was fully God and therefore not man at all; the apparent human nature was not real.

OUT WITH THE OLD, AND IN WITH THE NEW[3]

Marcion said, "Apostles? Just Paul;
New and old Gods aren't the same at all."
Tertullian said his
Antitheses is
A testament to being heretical.

CLANGING SYMBOLS?

From passages where skeptics give grief,
Symbolism is a short cut to relief.
But figurative use
Invites abuse—
The Origen of some odd beliefs.

GOVERNMENT HEALTH PLANS

Constantine made a big stir.
With a new sign he'd be conqueror.
He won more and more,
His men were less sore,
For he was a chi-rho practicer.

3. Marcionianism was an early second century heresy which claims that the creator and redeemer Gods are different, and that Paul was the only true apostle (while ignoring much of his writing). Marcion's *Antitheses* was a work in which he tried to make the Old and New Testaments contradict each other.

UNREASONABLE REASONING

Human logic can only carry us
So far, and may be nefarious.
"God both one and three?
Why that just couldn't be!"
Thus went the false reason of Arius.

WHAT'S IN YOUR STOCKING?

I said "homo*i*ousios" and he punched me so quick
That I knew in a moment he must be St. Nick.[4]
How to not be naughty?
It is quite easy to see:
The Nicea list has no heretic.

CREATED CONTROVERSY

Ink on the creed was scarcely dry,
When for overruling they did try.
The emperor's will carryin'
Folks to be Arian:
No more Mr. Nicea Guy.[5]

---

4. The historicity of the claim that Nicholas hit Arius is rather doubtful, though. For that matter, the term homoiousios came into use some time after Nicea. Nicholas of Myra had no sleigh or reindeer, either—as Chico Marx stated, "There ain't no sanity clause." (Wood, *Night*)

5. Despite the decision at Nicea, Arian or semi-Arian views gained widespread and sometimes imperial support at points over the next decades, resulting in several exiles of Athanasius.

DO-NOT-ISTS?

When the lapsed sought to re-enter,
The debates caused churches to splinter.
"You're not of the chosen,
For on watch, you were doughzin'!
Our rivals had a hole in the center."[6]

FRUITFUL THINKING

From Augustine's insight we are heirs,
For his absconding with pears
Became food for thought—
Not doing what he ought
With friends out to grab what's not theirs.

GREEN WISEACRES

He used shamrocks to ensure
Comprehension. The Irish were
So impressed, then and there
They gave him a chair
On the lawn—Paddy O' Furniture.

6. After Constantine ended official persecution, the church faced the prob-
lem of how to handle those who had recanted their faith under persecution,
but now sought to return to the church. The party advocating continued exclu-
sion of the compromisers became known as the Donatists (though from the
start there were other theological issues, class, ethnicity, and politics mixed
into the controversy). The post-sermon coffee break may have been invented
by Donutists, who may be at risk of hole-ier than thou attitudes. Donatus's
rival was Caecilian, which might suggest connections to the underground
church. (Caecilians are worm-like, legless, burrowing amphibians.)

FOR GOODNESS' SNAKES

In the land of the northwestern Celt,
A surplus of reptiles was felt.
Pat used holy clout
To drive them all out,[7]
After buckling each serpentine belt.

TURN OFF THE PHONE

Pope Gregory oft bemoaned all
The congregants checking for a phone call.
Instead of a rant,
He invented a chant[8]
Because it was anti-phonal.

CLAST CRUSADE[9]

Were icons devotional fixtures?
Or eye cons, idolatrous mixtures?
Do the images click?
Or a heathen trick?
Both sides sought to get all the pictures.

7. It was actually not hard to drive the snakes out, as there weren't any—the glaciers had already eliminated them.

8. Actually, "Gregorian Chant" is later in origin than Gregory, though he may have promoted some of the early work that led towards it. The reader is likely to notice another anachronism in the limerick as well.

9. The iconoclast movement in Eastern Orthodoxy sought to eliminate the use of images.

DUE PROCESS

For heresy, they needed a test;
Unilateral creed change wasn't best.
Inserting *filioque*[10]
Just wasn't OK.
It helped to split up East and West.

CAROL PERIL

Duke Václav converted, no doubt,
But his rule seemed lacking in clout.
Boleslav, his brother,
Nominated another—
Good King Wenceslaus, look out![11]

MUDDLE IN THE CATHEDRAL

Church might—Henry sought how to check it.
A plan, but Tom's conscience could wreck it.
When his pal sought to be
Archbishop properly,
The king then sought to kick the Beckett.

---

10. "and from the Son." The Nicene Creed originally stated that the Spirit proceeds from the Father. The western church (under Rome) encountered an error that could be ruled out by adding this phrase to the creed. However, modifying the creed without a church council was a bad idea. Conversely, the Eastern Orthodox attempts to argue that the Spirit doesn't exactly proceed from the Son also are somewhat strained.

11. Although Václav's grandfather was the first Czech leader to convert to Christianity, his mother returned to her pagan roots and got exiled. Václav firmly established Christianity among the people, but he was not adept at dealing with foreign powers. Boleslav had him assassinated (reportedly participating in the murder), but continued the support of Christianity. Václav's name was garbled into Wenceslaus by the time it got to England.

ARISTOTLE MODEL

Aquinas looked slow, but thought quicker.[12]
A mental heavyweight, not a slicker.
Hard problems he sought,
Then wrestled in thought,
Thus was called Sumo Theologica.[13]

UNDER STUDY

Pondering where unbaptized good go
Led to the idea of Limbo,
But if what we inherit
Is based on our merit,
That's setting the bar very low.

A PRAGUEMATIC APPROACH

The congregants on reform were hooked,
So on many charges Hus was booked.
He knew without doubt,
They'd try to Czech out.
His teaching lasts, though his goose[14] was cooked.

---

12. His classmates disparagingly called him the ox, but when Thomas finally did speak up they were cowed by his superior grasp of the material.

13. Not mud wrestling, though—one's wallow does not a Summa make. (Aristotle, *Nicomachean*, 1.7, 1098 [standard reference numbering; p. 13 in the translation cited])

14. Hus is Czech for goose.

NEEDING A HERO

From his studies, Martin was sure:
Salvation by grace was truth, for
He tried following law
'Til he clearly saw
No hope in being a *lex* Luther.[15]

WITH BEATLED BROW . . .

"Faith without works is dead?" he stewed.
"An epistle of straw, I conclude!"[16]
If that also did cover
James' little brother,
Luther could have called him a Hay Jude.

WURST-KÄSE SCENARIO?

We must never emulate
Satan in his cruel hate.
From this one sees
Not to shred cheap cheese,
For one learns that his Kraft is grate.

15. "Lex": law (Latin). Lex Luthor is among the more prominent of villains who haven't read enough comic books to realize that Superman will win every time.

16. Martin Luther, as an occasional theologian (*i.e.*, focusing on particular issues as they arose), found James' wording problematic with regard to *sola fide*. A more systematic approach to theology fits James 2:14–26 with Romans 4 by seeing that James addresses the error of empty profession of faith—in Pauline words, James is saying that true faith will have fruit, not that our works achieve salvation. The claim "I have faith" is justified by reference to the fruit of good works, but the sinner is justified by faith.

THE BIG CHEESE?[17]

"God will come in Münster,"[18] he said.
Jan Matthys in battle was dead.
As history lists,
The Anabaptists
Should have stopped when they got a head.

PAT EXAMPLES[19]

Jan of Leyden then sought to create
A communal, polygamist state.
The Patriarchs gave
The example he craved
To get himself more than one mate.

17. Munster or muenster is an Alsatian cheese.

18. The Münster Rebellion or Anabaptist Kingdom of Münster was a millenarian Anabaptist attempt to control Münster, because their leader Jan Matthys said that that would be the location of the second coming and institution of the millennium in 1534 or 1535. Jan Matthys's predecessor in leadership, Melchior Hoffman, had believed that this would happen in Strasbourg in 1533, and went there to try to convert the town to his ideas; instead he got arrested for his statements that the sinners needed to be purged from the city. Jan Matthys claimed the same things about purging sinners in order to make the city more welcoming for the second coming, and forcibly converted Münster to Anabaptism (convert, leave, or be executed).

Jan Matthys' head was mounted on a pike after he was killed when, believing he and those who followed him were under God's protection, he led a sortie on Easter Sunday, 1534, against the former Bishop of Münster's besieging forces.

A desire not to be associated with events like these is part of the original reason why most of the Dutch remnants of the Anabaptists, led by Menno, were not millenarian and emphasized being pacifistic.

19. Jan Matthys' successor, Jan of Leyden (and to a lesser extent Jan Matthys), used patriarchal examples to try to turn Münster into a communal, polygamist theocracy (not to be confused with the Taborite communal polyamorist theocracies of the 1300s).

RAD BELIEFS[20]

Radical Spiritualists say, "We
Trust direct revelation only."
"No source of spiritual
Truth is material."
They're followed by much of modernity.

RATIONALITY AND THE THREE PERSONS[21]

"It's not true if I don't think it's reasonable,
And I think the Bible's totally literal."
These seem contradictory,
But both claims were key
To be 'Evangelically Rational.'

QUEEN OF NOTS

Once reform had opened the locks,
Absolutism was in for some shocks.
Threats from Mary
Just weren't scary
When he'd been through the school of hard Knox.[22]

20. The Radical Spiritualists were an early 16th century radical reformation movement which rejected all ceremonies, sacraments, and organized religion and all authorities other than the direct revelation to one's Inner Spirit. They also went in for the gnostic "physical bad, spiritual good" view. They believed that those and only those who had this inner spirit were saved, and that those who had it were infallible in regards to what very little doctrine was left. Some of the leaders of the peasants in the German Peasant War of 1524–25 were socially extreme, millenarian, Radical Spiritualists.

21. Evangelical Rationalists were individuals like Servetus and Socinus that said that only beliefs which accorded with human reason and a hyper-literal reading of the Bible were true. Their most emphasized views were anti-Trinitarianism and denial of the divinity of Christ.

22. Despite the harsh treatment he had endured, and the fact that Mary Queen of Scots was closely tied to the leading French persecutors of Protestants, Knox's responses to Mary's demands largely consisted of simply ignoring them.

A POINT-SHAVING SCHEME

Arminius sought to decline
To follow a full Reformed line.
He tried to fashion
More room for our passion,
Thus the making of Calvin *klein*.[23]

"NOBODY EXPECTS THE VENETIAN INQUISITION"[24]

"Everyone's backward who doesn't agree
With my complex, mystical theology!"[25]
'Twas sufficient offense.
It wasn't "science"[26]
That got Bruno's works banned in 1603.[27]

23. *Klein*: Dutch (and German) for "little." It shows that Arminius didn't get the point—he was tiptoeing away from TULIP.

24. In 1591, Bruno received an invitation to instruct a Venetian patrician in memory, and went to Venice. After two months, his pupil denounced him to the local inquisition. The Venetian inquisition was inclined to disbelieve the charges until they were informed of the proceeding that had been started against him in 1576 for defending some of Arius's views in the margins of a copy of Erasmus's (banned) works. After lengthy negotiations, Bruno was sent to the Roman Inquisition in 1593.

25. The combination of anti-Aristotelian views; beliefs in theurgistic magic, reincarnation, Hermetic mysticism, and various heresies like non-trinitarianism and denial of the virgin birth; along with conceitedness, a penchant for referring to himself in the third person as a genius, and calling everyone who disagreed with him backward and ignorant; got Bruno kicked out of Naples, Geneva, Oxford, Paris, Wittenberg, and Helmstedt, in that order. Fighting between Protestants and Catholics drove him out of Toulouse (to London and Oxford) and London (to Paris).

26. The popular claim that Bruno was a martyr for science and free speech is a nineteenth-century myth. He did believe in heliocentrism, an infinite universe, and a plurality of worlds with life on them; however, his bizarre, non-scientific mysticism and "I have everything figured out by philosophy" views put him distinctly outside of modern science. Likewise, he favored free speech for himself and everyone else being free to agree with him, not freedom for all views.

27. All of Bruno's writings were placed on the *Index Librorum Prohibitorum*,

GEO OR EGOCENTRIC?

Bruno argued with vigor and vim
That all men must agree with him.
It became evident
That he wouldn't repent,
Which made chance of reprieve very slim.[28]

1611 AND ALL THAT

From reform, James sought a diversion
To cast on Calvinist claims aspersion.
"No divine right of kings?
Who writes these things?"
That's how it goes in his own version.[29]

---

becoming, for Roman Catholics, Bruno no-nos.

28. The Inquisition, at the time, let you off the first time if you admitted that you were wrong and promised not to do it again. After Bruno apologized, but before he could be released, fellow prisoners complained of his efforts to push his weird ideas on them. This damaged the credibility of his professed repentance.

29. Reformed teaching, exemplified by the footnotes in the popular Geneva version of the Bible, emphasized the responsibilities of rulers to obey God and the duty of the people to reject a ruler who did not fulfill his theological duties. James didn't like how such views had led to his mother, Mary Queen of Scots, not getting her way in Scotland. (Oddly, not getting her way in Scotland seemed to rankle James more than her getting executed in England.) He therefore wanted a new translation to replace the Geneva. Some publishers helpfully copied the Geneva footnotes over into their editions of the King James Version, defeating James's purpose in supporting a new translation. His son Charles I tried to implement James' ideas about absolute monarchy, an effort that went over poorly.

PILGRIMS' DIGRESS

Channel crossing some freedom did bring,
But distractions proved quite enticing.
"Westward we'll bear—
Faith may flower there!"
For the Pilgrims found Leiden most jarring.[30]

NOT A BLIND DATE

Ussher did not seek to create a
Final word, but compiled all data.
As rocks came in view,
The numbers grew,
Though precise calculations came later.[31]

A WORD IN SEASON

From reading many books, great and small,
October twenty-third's Ussher's call.
The message he's carryin'
Is supralapsarian,[32]
For mankind began in the fall.

30. A Leiden jar was an early device enabling one to study electricity much more conveniently and safely than Franklin's lightning experiment. However, that is not what the Pilgrim leaders found shocking about the culture.

31. The 17th century chronologers such as James Ussher and Isaac Newton compiled all the historical data available (particularly from the Bible but also what was known from classical sources) in building a history of the world. Following their example, the early geologists supplemented written history records with evidence from the rocks. Gradually, geological discoveries were accepted as indicating that the Bible passed over a long pre-human series of events because it was theologically unimportant. This was not seen as any problem for the reliability of the Bible. On the contrary, the picture from geology of a large but finite age to the earth and directional trends in the history of life were promoted as supporting the Bible against the infinite cycles favored by many "Enlightenment" deists and atheists.

32. Eschatology fans call this "pre-rib."

NO LAUD OR HONOR[33]

"Laudian worship the Scots will now get."
At "Beauty of Holiness," they were upset.
Stools at Hannay were shot,
Then two wars were fought
For the beauty of no bishops yet.

CONSCIENCE OBJECTORS[34]

The Ranters their conscience trusted
As their only way to be led.
Their peers frowned upon
These tenets anon
As an excuse to paint the town red.

33. The first and second Bishops' Wars (1639 & 1640), fought between the Covenanter Army (later to become involved in the English Civil Wars) and Charles I's army were touched off by the introduction of Laudian Anglican worship and an adapted version of the English Book of Common Prayer into Scottish churches.

The first use of the new prayer book was in St. Giles Cathedral, in Edinburgh. James Hannay, the Archbishop of Edinburgh, began to read the collects. In response, one or a few lower-class women near the front of the congregation said something which condemned this as a mass, then threw a stool at Hannay. This precipitated a general riot in which the congregants threw most things which were not held in place (more stools, Bibles, rocks, etc.) at the archbishop as he was on his way out. Similar scenes forcing most Anglican-affiliated Scottish ministers to hide in city chambers did not really fulfill what Laud and Charles meant by the "Beauty of Holiness" (i.e., "Beauty of being a good Laudian Anglican").

34. The Ranters (along with the Muggletonians, Quakers, and Fifth Monarchy Men) were a group of religious radicals that sprang up in England in the 1650s. Bucholz states that the Ranters believed that "sin" is only sin if your conscience convicts you of it: "Any act which is done in light and love, is light and lovely, even if it may be called..." (Bucholz, *England*, Lecture 33). This prompted the Rump Parliament to pass acts against drunkenness, adultery, swearing, and blasphemy.

WE'RE SAVED! WAIT, NOW HE SAYS WE'RE NOT?[35]

Muggleton was put in the pen
For "being a prophet 'mong men."
When he wasn't jailed,
His followers hailed
That he could save or damn right then.

QUAKERS FEELING THEIR OATS[36]

Quakers from nobles oft got some spite.
For they disliked Quakers' great "inner light."
"It would make all equal!
And they won't give us full
Humble deference, nor deign to fight."

35. The Muggletonians held that their eponymous leader (a former tanner) was the last prophet foretold in Revelation and so, because of this, he had the power to save or damn a person on the spot (thus, these declarations were tan lines). He did so publicly in the 1650s, when he wasn't imprisoned for blasphemy.

36. The Quakers said that all people have an equal measure of "inner light." This meant that giving deference (e.g. tipping one's cap or giving the wall) to those of higher status was wrong. Most Quakers were also pacifists.

MOSAIC OF IDEAS[37]

"Four kingdoms from Daniel are dead;
The fifth one is Jesus," they said.
"We must force it through
With hullabaloo!
To impose Moses' laws we are led."

COGITO EGO SUM

Said a confident Enlightenment deist,
"From action God surely would desist,
For that in my eyes
Is the way of the wise."
Thus showing that he's really a me-ist.

METH-ODD?[38]

Wesley sought to avoid a schism,
But his reforms led to a division:
"Preach in fields to people,
Not just near a steeple?!
There's madness to his methodism!"[39]

37. The Fifth Monarchy Men looked at the end times predictions in Daniel and thought, "Four of the monarchies have come and gone and the fifth one is obviously Jesus' kingdom, so the Commonwealth is an interim, and the Second Coming is imminent." To prepare, they believed that obeying English Common Law was a sin, and that they needed to impose Mosaic Law on England (as seriously discussed by the Parliament of Saints in 1653); some said that the Second Coming needed to be brought to occurrence by force (i.e., "Proclaiming King Jesus in the middle of London will make him come down from heaven"). It didn't work.

38. An "Adopt a Highway" sign near the north end of the county that we're in credits the "United Meth Men." Changing the abbreviation might be a good idea.

39. His brother Charles's high reputation as a hymnwriter contrasts with their father's fondness for writing bad poems on topics ill-suited for poetic

THESES AND ANTITHESES

"Right versus wrong"—that concept's not hard.[40]
But to Hegel, such a dichotomy jarred.
A call to synthesize[41]
Can smooth over lies.[42]
Against this, keep the Kirk on guard.

MISSING THE TRAIN[ING]

Few seminarians were in the great outdoors,
But with folks moving out west in scores,
Quick ordination
By each congregation
Led to taking greener pastors.[43]

---

commemoration, such as "On a Supper of Stinking Ducks" and "Pindaricque on the Grunting of a Hog." Despite the considerable differences in style, the present compilation may have some of the senior Wesley's poetic spirit and skill.

40. Of course, humans and their endeavors contain a mix of both.

41. Although Hegel is popularly associated with the thesis + antithesis = synthesis sequence (see, *e.g.*, Taylor, *Porcine*, 48), he neither originated it nor emphasized it himself, focusing rather on the issue of contradictions inherent within any one concept or category.

42. Hegel's system of history was an inspiration for later systems of history such as Marx's or fascism's. Asserting that history follows a simple pattern such as proposed in any of these ideas requires ignoring the actual facts of history.

43. A major issue in the U.S. associated with the Second Great Awakening, though similar issues arise wherever churches are spreading into areas remote from established churches. Debates about handling the situation and about the appropriateness of some of the more sensational aspects of frontier revivals led to splits such as the Old School/New School Presbyterians.

RECALCULATING

He thought that he had the knack
To calculate Christ's return track.
Instead, the Lord sent
Great disappointment.
Miller[44] could not find a good come back.

TRANSCENDING MEANING

Though your search may be quite Thoreau,
Finding meaning may prove very slow.
If for logic you seek,
You could read all week
And still be asking, "Where's Waldo?"[45]

44. William Miller, in the early 1840s, interpreted Daniel to conclude that Christ would return within the next few years. His teaching with the "I can interpret the Bible for myself without regard for training or the wisdom of others" principle was very popular, attracting many followers. Less cautious than Miller's initial approach, some of his followers calculated an exact date of return, and eventually swayed Miller. Their initial prediction was revised, but when nothing happened in October 1844, the movement broke up as followers returned to more conventional teaching, dropped out, or devised their own sects to explain the discrepancy. Seventh-day Adventism and Jehovah's Witnesses emerged out of the last option.

45. Hawthorne, "Railroad," 223 and Poe, "Blackwood," 126–127 parodied transcendentalism as nonsense. ["Moneypenny" in the latter comes from the Em- of Emerson; many other of Poe's humorous stories also mock transcendentalism, but often rather obscurely to the modern reader.]

LIVELY REVIVING?

Finney[46] sought many large crowds to win,
But lasting fruit from this was thin.
Sustained excite
Took all his might—
Nightly he's Barnum again.

APPARENTLY NOT?

Gosse worked hard on his scheme, but few were
Impressed. Yet science won't be disprover:
Though he seems at sea,
It physically
Matches through his navel maneuver.[47]

A NIETZSCHE MARKET

"Of Christ don't keep even an inch!
Be as heartless as an unreformed Grinch!
Force each poor go-fer
To work as your chauffeur!
That's the way to become an *Übermensch*."[48]

---

46. Charles Grandison Finney, the most famous of preachers in the Second Great Awakening due to his efforts to win converts through excitement. Even he admitted that this didn't seem to produce very lasting effects.

47. Gosse, *Omphalos* developed an elaborate system of apparent history, the title (though not the contents) anticipating Boynton, *Belly*. Gosse's title alludes to the fact that Adam and Eve would be created directly *ex nihlo* with navels in his scenario. Although creation with apparent history raises significant theological and philosophical problems, it is compatible with any possible physical evidence. In contrast, trying to find scientific evidence to support a young earth has been completely unsuccessful scientifically but much more popular with the public than Gosse's approach.

48. Nietzsche affirmed the inconsistency of picking and choosing parts of Christianity (such as in the "Enlightenment" thinking that underlies most current Western sociopolitical systems), and advocated throwing out all traces of

GENEROUSLY FUNDED

Clear doctrine, not a vague mist,
Is needed to forestall a wrong twist.
Yet we should steer wide
Of wrongful divide
Don't pad your fundamental list.[49]

WHO'S RIGHT?

Inerrancy's problem is apparent:
The topic of many an unfair rant.
Pro or con, we soon see,
For all too many,
It's themselves that they view as inerrant.[50]

Christianity. He largely failed to notice the problem of his own claims that it is right to deny that right and wrong exist. As is typical of claims to disbelieve in absolutes, his affirmation that the *Übermensch* would show his superiority by imposing a self-created moral system proves on inspection to be treating Nietzsche's own preferences as absolutes. "I can do whatever I want, and you can do whatever I want."

49. Although "fundamentalist" today labels either extremists or those that we want to portray as extremist, properly it should refer to one who is committed to the fundamentals of something, in contrast to a nominal adherent. Extremists actually tend to have a poor grasp of the fundamentals, often focusing on certain details while missing the big picture.

50. Fans of inerrancy too often insist that their interpretation is the unquestionable word of God, while those opposing it rarely question their own judgment in assessing the supposed flaws of the Bible. Both tend to treat the Bible as a collection of proof texts to be assessed by modern fashions of historical reporting rather than as a unified whole written using the conventions of ancient Near Eastern cultures. Inerrancy of the Bible should inspire a careful effort to understand what it means, by its own standards.

SOURCE-ERY

Is this verse J, P, E, or D?
The choice is all yours, you see.
And as for the date,
Just say that it's late,
If a modernist critic you'd be.

PSEUDEPITAPHS[51]

If to the text, you have an aversion,
On authorship you could cast aspersion.
Each book would be
A forgery
In this un-author-ized version.

WHO MET A PAIR OF ORTHODOX?

To liberalism, he gave many shocks,
Yet Barth wasn't in conservative flocks.
"Neoorthodoxy"
Is contradictory;
It's more apt to call it para-dox.[52]

51. Pseudepigraphia is a technical term for fictional authorship. Some claims to identify parts of the Bible as pseudepigraphia seem to presume epitaphs for sound scholarship.

52. Ortho-: straight, true. Para-: beside. -dox: opinion; praise. In chemistry, if two additional parts are attached onto a six-carbon ring, straight across is ortho-, adjacent is para-, and having one carbon in between the two attached parts is meta-.

UMPIRE STRIKES BACK

When on text as a judge he does sit,
There's very little that's left of it.
What he's displeased with
Is dismissed as a myth
For he thinks that it's not a hit.

WISE USE OF MEANS

Though flashy preaching's oft a sham,
Those on TV aren't all flimflam.
What quickly sends
The Word to the ends
Of the Earth? Use a telly, Graham.

NEW WAVE

On style, many take rigid stands.
"Contemporary?" "What type of bands?"
But becoming charismatic
Is not automatic:
It depends on a show of hands.

A MIDAS TOUCH?

From fleeced followers, the cash flow
To prosperity preachers does go.
As they seek the divine
Merely as a cash mine,[53]
They're left, still waiting for God dough.[54]

CALIBRATE GOOD TIMES

Omride, not David's dynasty,
Stands out in low chronology.
Archaeology's layers
And 14C are naysayers
To this minimalist theology.[55]

---

53. In contrast to liberation theology, which sees theology as justifying you or the government going after the cash, or the complacent "capitalism is great" popular theology of those who already have the cash. Capitalism's main merit as an economic theory is that it works, but biblical principles require regulating capitalism to protect the public, the workers, *etc.*

54. Though at least the followers generally get some entertaining theatrics from prosperity preaching, unlike those watching boring existentialist non-action plays.

55. It is true that the Bible passes over the impressive power and wealth of the northern kingdom under Omri and Ahab, focusing on their theological failings instead, and that the culturally appropriate rhetoric used in the Bible regarding the united monarchy can give exaggerated ideas when read literalistically by a modern reader. (For example, allies giving tribute are included in the extent of the kingdom, as well as the area actually under full control by David or Solomon.) However, assigning all of the major building work in Israel to the ninth century BC or later is not realistic. Carbon dating and magnetic field measurements place a widespread destruction layer, affecting previously impressive cities, to about 930 BC, for example. This matches Shishak's raid on Rehoboam and Jeroboam, demonstrating major building work somewhat earlier in the tenth century BC, *i.e.*, during Solomon's time. Several other archaeological problems likewise show that the claim that no archaeological trace exists of the united monarchy is wrong (Kitchen, *Reliability*, 139–158; Bruins et al., "Tel Rehov," 315–318; Vaknina et al., "Geomagnetic," 4).

BIBLIOGRAPHY

Abingdon, Alexander. *The Omnibus Boners*. New York: Blue Ribbon, 1931.

Aristotle. *Nicomachean Ethics*. Translated by Robert C. Bartlett and Susan D. Collins. 2011. Chicago: University of Chicago Press.

Benson, Donald R. *Biblical Limericks*. New York: Ballantine, 1986.

Boynton, Sandra. *Belly Button Book*. New York: Workman, 2005.

Bruins, Hendrik J., et al. "14C Dates from Tel Rehov: Iron-Age Chronology, Pharaohs, and Hebrew Kings." *Science* 300 (2003) 315–18. https://doi.org/10.1126/science.1082776

Bucholz, Robert. *A History of England from the Tudors to the Stuarts*. Chantilly, VA: Great Courses, 2003.

Bulwer-Lytton, Edward. *Paul Clifford*. London: Colburn and Bentley, 1830.

Byron, George Gordon. "The Destruction of Sennacherib." In *Hebrew Melodies*, 46. London: John Murray, 1815. [Original title spelled it Semnacherib, changed to Sennacherib in later editions.]

Carroll, Lewis. *The Annotated Alice*. New York: Random House, 1998.

Clowney, Edmund P. *Eutychus (and His Pin)*. Grand Rapids: Eerdmans, 1960.

Doyle, Arthur Conan. "The Adventure of the Naval Treaty." In *The Original Illustrated Sherlock Holmes*, 305–26. Secaucus, NJ: Castle, 1981.

———. *A Study in Scarlet and The Sign of the Four*. New York: Berkley, 1975.

Gilliam, Terry, and Terry Jones, dir. *Monty Python and the Holy Grail*. Burbank, CA: Columbia Tristar Home Video, 1991. VHS.

Gosse, Philip Henry. *Omphalos: An Attempt to Untie the Geological Knot*. London: Van Voorst, 1857.

Harvey, Allan H. *Thoughts on "Joshua's Long Day."* 2009. http://steamdoc.itgo.com/writings/joshua.html

Hawthorne, Nathaniel. "The Celestial Railroad." In *The Comic Tradition in America*, edited by Kenneth S. Lynn, 214–31. New York: Doubleday, 1958.

Irving, Washington. "The Legend of Sleepy Hollow." In *The Sketch Book of Geoffrey Crayon, Gent.*, 453–98. New York: Putnam and Son, 1868.

Keats, John. "La Belle Dame sans Merci." In *The Poems of John Keats*, 244–47. New York: Dodd, Mead, 1905.

———. "Ode on a Grecian Urn." In *The Poems of John Keats*, 194–95. New York: Dodd, Mead, 1905.

Kitchen, K. A. *On the Reliability of the Old Testament.* Grand Rapids: Eerdmans, 2003.

Lewis, Clive Staples. *The Screwtape Letters.* New York: MacMillan, 1961.

Nawrocki, Mike, dir. *Larry's Wonderful World of Autotainment.* Burbank, CA: Warner Home Video, 2003. VHS.

Nash, Ogden. "The Strange Case of Mr. Ballantine's Valentine." In *I'm a Stranger Here Myself*, 77–79. Boston: Little, Brown, 1938.

————. "Very Like a Whale." In *Verses from 1929 On*, 23–24. Boston, Little, Brown, 1959.

Poe, Edgar Allan. "How to Write a Blackwood Article." In *Edgar Allan Poe: Selected Works*, 126–32. New York: Gramercy, 1985.

Roberts, Brian, dir. *Moe and the Big Exit.* Nashville: Word Entertainment, 2007. DVD.

Sayers, Dorothy L. "The Bibulous Business of a Matter of Taste." In *Lord Peter*, 154–67. New York: Harper & Row, 1987.

Sellar, Walter Carruthers, and Robert Julian Yeats. *1066 and All That.* New York: Barnes & Noble, 1993.

Shakespeare, William. "Julius Casear." In *The Riverside Shakespeare*, 1100–134. Boston: Houghton Mifflin, 1974.

Taylor, James. *The Quintessential Porcine History of Philosophy and Religion.* Nashville: Abingdon, 1972.

Tennyson, Alfred. "Lady Clara Vere de Vere." In *Poems*, 155–58. London: Edward Moxton, 1842.

Twain, Mark. "The Innocents Abroad." In *The Unabridged Mark Twain*, 11-389. Philadelphia: Running, 1976.

Vakina, Yoav, et al. "Reconstructing Biblical Military Campaigns Using Geomagnetic Field Data." *Proceedings of the National Academy of Science* 119 (2022) e2209117119. https://doi.org/10.1073/pnas.2209117119

Wodehouse, Pelham G. "Ukridge's Dog College." In *Ukridge*, 11–33. New York: Overlook, 1924.

————. *Life with Jeeves.* New York: Penguin, 1981.

Wood, Sam, director. *A Night at the Opera.* Metro-Goldwyn-Mayer, 1935.